Spirit Healing

Spirit Healing
Native American
Magic & Medicine

Mary Dean Atwood
Illustrated by Bert Seabourn

 Sterling Publishing Co., Inc. New York

Library of Congress Cataloging-in-Publication Data

Atwood, Mary Dean.
  Spirit healing : native American magic and medicine / by Mary Dean
Atwood.
    p.   cm.
  Includes index.
  ISBN 0-8069-8266-7
  1. Magic—United States.   2. Medicine, Magic, mystic, and
spagiric—United States.   3. Indians of North America—Magic.
4. Indians of North America—Medicine.   5. Indians of North America—
Religion and mythology.   6. Spiritual life.   7. Spiritual healing.
I. Title.
BF1622.U6A78   1991
299'.75—dc20   91–21220
                                                                    CIP

Published in 1991 by Sterling Publishing Company, Inc.
387 Park Avenue South, New York, N.Y. 10016
© 1991 by Mary Dean Atwood
Illustrations © 1991 by Bert Seabourn
Distributed in Canada by Sterling Publishing
% Canadian Manda Group, P.O. Box 920, Station U
Toronto, Ontario, Canada M8Z 5P9
Distributed in Great Britain and Europe by Cassell PLC
Villiers House, 41/47 Strand, London WC2N 5JE, England
Distributed in Australia by Capricorn Link Ltd.
P.O. Box 665, Lane Cove, NSW 2066
Manufactured in the United States of America
All rights reserved

Sterling ISBN 0-8069-8266-7

DEDICATION

This book is dedicated to all my teachers, wherever they are, including:

Bernard Jensen, Loretta Bonebright, Gary Young, Jacooba, Byron Gentry, Theta Starr, Wahanee, Sunne Eagle Woman Nelson, Gloria Star, Jerry Denson, Gary Bear Heals, Liliah, Robert White Eagle Browning, Gabriel, Ann Always In The Middle Shadlow, Anne and Paxton Robey, Bonne Fink, Inez Bubbles Wyrick, Veronica Winkler, Lee Sexton, Ching Chow Eee, Eileen Nauman, Michael Harner, and Pheenatoon.

ACKNOWLEDGMENTS

A special thank-you to Sheila Anne Barry who first suggested the birth of this book and saw it through to completion. Appreciation is due to the Sterling Publishing staff for their help in developing this project.

I also thank friend Kathryn Fanning for her superb editing skills and support. Without Jean Tucker at the word processor, the manuscript would probably still be on my desk. She also offered creative assistance.

I want to acknowledge Bert Seabourn for his beautiful art work and for helping Bushyhead and Little Hummingbird come alive, and again extend my gratitude to my Native American teachers and to my friends on the Red Path for their inspiration and encouragement.

Lastly, I want to mention my children, Denise and Douglas, who have always believed in their mother, and give thanks to my parents for their aid and support.

Contents

Color illustrations are found after page 64

FOREWORD

I grew up on the RoseBud reservation in South Dakota. I still spend time there during the Bear Heals Sun Dance and off and on during the year when I am not traveling. I have taken part in eighteen Sun Dances, conducting eleven of them myself. I travel around to wherever I am needed, performing sweat lodges and vision quests.

My grandfather learned his medicine from Big Owl, a medicine man. Red men of the past had greater knowledge of the truths. Since that time has come a complexity and mixing of the truths that has changed thoughts and actions and brought a different type of beauty. The Red Man has not been free to learn in traditional fashion. But the root in the Tree of Life is again starting to grow. Black Elk believed that this root will grow into a tree. The old ways of knowledge will return.

Mary Atwood has arrived on the Red Path by different trails and teachers, but at some point in our journey, it was time for us to meet. She happened to be looking for a Native American teacher in order to expand her knowledge of the ways of the spirit. The fact that her fictional character Bushyhead had Bear as a power animal, that she wore a bear claw necklace, and that my name is Gary Bear Heals demonstrates the order of seeming coincidences awaiting those on the path. Her carved bear fetish disappeared shortly before she attended my first sweat lodge.

Dr. Atwood has an ability to seek the esoteric, indefinable spiritual world through the use of exercises and practices. She is sensitive to the nature of the Native American Spirit in her characters and is a student of the truth. This book is the first step to awaken the mind to the existence of another world that offers peace and harmony. We of the Bear Heals family believe it to be a significant contribution. Waste (pronounced wash–tay, meaning done well).

—Gary Bear Heals
Lakota Spiritual Teacher

Introduction

Inspiration for this book, both story and procedures, has come from the hologram of my existence. Included are research findings, personal experiences, observations, teachings from Native Americans and institutional data derived from my own experiences as a contemporary medicine woman. This list is incomplete unless mention be made of knowledge given from sources not easily named as they come from other planes of existence.

The incidents related in this book are generic with regard to tribe, place, and anecdotes. Although some events have been patterned from research material of people and events, there is no emphasis on one particular group or regional location. My research favors the Plains, Great Basin, Southwest and California culture areas.

The book attempts to capture the sacred nature of Native Americans, so rich in spirit and soul. In doing so, an overlap will be noted with other religions or ways of life that stress the same things. Unlike Western spirituality, the Native American lived religion everyday—it was a way of life. Like Eastern religious philosophies, the spirit or soul of the person was considered foremost. A person's spiritual essence was not limited to three-dimensional time and space. Depending upon how highly developed a person was, he or she was free to transcend into the future or to view the past. Both the medicine person and the holy person from India note the existence of realities unknown to many Americans of European descent. The ability to call on spiritual energy and power for healing or creation still exists today.

By comparison, Western religion essentially ignores the divine immortal aspect of humans—the spirit. The spirit takes more significance when viewed as transcending lives as well as time and space. Despite the fact that the Christian Bible is full of references to the soul going on to join the heavenly Father, one's current life is seen as a one-shot existence. Though the experiences of biblical prophets and healers are reported in the Bible, little credence is given to people using those skills today.

The Native American, like followers of Eastern religions, believed that all animal, mineral, and plant life contained a spiritual essence or living force. Current research of the examination of DNA in modern Native Americans suggests that North and South American Indians came from one culture in Asia that migrated across the Bering Strait. This link explains the similarity between the Eastern religious philosophies and those of the Native Americans. The spiritual link between these two great ancient ways of life again stresses the importance of human soul growth as the reason for existence. This divine spark is shared by other forms of nature.

To destroy the other life forms on the planet is to invite your own destruction. The recent necessity for planetary and wildlife ecology has brought this ancient wisdom to the attention of Western thinking. Our divine energy is connected to the energy of other forms of life. The realization of this wisdom intuitively perceived by Native Americans will become more obvious as humans cope with the destruction that they have brought to the planet.

The best-documented existence of spiritual helpers and proof of life after death has come from the near-death experiences of survivors. Interestingly, a shaman typically has such an experience before he or she receives power. One of my Native American teachers met with the Owl Woman who lives on a star during his near-death experience. He was told that he had to return to earth because he had not done what he needed to do.

Other people, including myself, have been privileged to see, hear, or feel into the unseen dimensions through vision quests or spirit communications. Proof is important for the Western mind. As the veil continues to thin between the concrete physical world and the esoteric spirit world, more evidence will be forthcoming for the disbelievers.

The notion of spirit teachers, such as the Grandmothers and the Grandfathers, inhabiting another world is accepted by the oldest religions of the world. Native Americans had relatives from the animal, nature, celestial, and human kingdoms, who often switched from one form to another as they desired or as lessons were accomplished. Restrictions of time and space were unknown although specific theories of transmigration were usually missing.

Some of the exercises in this book were channeled by Native American spirits. This is not a new phenomenon. White Eagle, channeled by Mrs. Grace Cooke of England, has been a popular source of spiritual inspiration in Europe for over fifty years as have the teachings of Silver Birch, a favorite of Lord Beaverbrook. The reason that many spirit guides have an Indian identity is because the Native Americans had a way of perceiving and living life in a circular as opposed to linear way, which kept them closer to divine power. Spirit entities take on specific heritages for teaching purposes, not because they need one on their planes of existence.

Defining "real" Native American practices turned out to be as difficult as trying to prove who are bona-fide Native Americans. In my research, I found that customs and beliefs vary from tribe to tribe. For example, the colors representing each of the four directions were different, but usually chosen from white, black, red, blue, or yellow. For this reason, it goes without saying that any reference to certain ways of doing rituals is only a guide and never the only way to do it.

In addition, Native Americans have the freedom to conceptualize religion in individual ways and do so. Two full-bloods from the same tribe may vary a great deal in their religious practices.

The identity of Native Americans is disputed. The government currently accepts as Native American a person with at least twenty-five percent Indian ancestry. The tribes vary widely in their assessment. Some of the Eastern tribes accept any person claiming to have Indian ancestry as a member of their rolls, much to the chagrin of the other tribes, inundated with medical privileges from these people.

Many Americans may have ancestral Indian blood that is unknown or not easily proven. The Native Americans were forced to take the names of other peoples when they signed the rolls. The names often were picked by the army supervisors. Thus, some Indians have the last name Sergeant. Such practices now make it virtually impossible to trace one's Native American ancestry. Many families, such as mine, suspect Indian heritage because the female ancestor had no last name.

More problems with genuine Indian traditions begin when one takes into account the tremendous efforts to which mainstream American culture has gone to eradicate all Indian religious practices. The missionaries, worried about saving the souls of Native Americans, successfully altered traditional ways over the centuries in which they worked with the Indians. The government did the same, but for other reasons. The Native Americans were forbidden to practice their ancient ways and dances because of fears of uprisings. Several hundred men, women, and children were killed at Wounded Knee when an attempt was made to have a Ghost Dance in 1890.

Perhaps the most changes have come from the incorporation of Native Americans into the mainstream world. In Oklahoma, where I reside, many of the leaders and politicians have Native American blood but few practice any traditions. Fortunately, some Native Americans and tribal leaders celebrate the traditions of old. Rarely a weekend goes by in Oklahoma that active tribal communities in small towns do not meet for a powwow or dance. The average person, with or without Indian ancestry, is either unaware or uninterested in these activities. Yet it has been fewer than ninety years since Oklahoma (Land of the Red Man), was officially part of Indian Territory!

The customs and belief systems of even full bloods are rarely what they were before the introduction of Christianity and later, relocation. Beliefs of my different full-blood Native American teachers vary widely. One of my teachers expressed sadness that the younger generation does not say its daily prayers facing the sun as she was brought up to do. However, when I asked if the sun was an entity or spirit to which the prayer paid homage, she seemed offended, saying that the prayer was to Jesus alone. This dear Native American, who embodies all that is pure and spiritual in thought and deed, was born in a teepee on a reservation in South Dakota, two decades after the incident at Wounded Knee.

Before the introduction of Christianity, spiritual deities, thought to exist in celestial bodies, ancestors, or the highest animal forms, were viewed as having power over the universe but were not always available for assistance. The lesser animal and nature spirits were sought as practical helpers necessary for one's well-being. The notion of one god, such as the Great White Father, is thought by some anthropologists to have resulted after the introduction of Christianity. However, most Native Americans believe that their religion acknowledged the existence of the one Great Spirit thousands of years before white men set foot on their soil. Their link with Eastern religion is proof of this.

The Eastern religions, which they may have shared at one time, profess the great all-knowing, all-powerful force within the universe. Westerners interpreted the many sacred forms within that power as separate deities instead of viewing them as different representations of a single energy.

The same reasoning was used by some anthropologists, who

thought that Native Americans worshiped many different gods. The various beings and spirits are manifestations of "one" power just as all of nature and its creatures on earth, share a "lesser" level. Because of that single sacred energy, Native Americans had no difficulty incorporating Jesus into their religious structure. Westerners, however, felt differently when asked to accept another's spiritual figures.

Most of my Native American teachers were brought up in various Western theologies, and they incorporated those traditions into their own religious practices. Others, such as the lady mentioned above, have had their original religious views eradicated. The majority have a mixed spiritual ideology.

My own interest in Native American traditions began with a series of experiences with bird and animal life which could be defined only in a Native American spiritual framework. I began to become aware of messages that were being given me by my bird and animal brothers and sisters, who could be defined as spirit helpers. There were no books or research on American Indians to describe this phenomenon. Fortunately, my attempt to understand what was happening increased my spiritual experiences. Usually one is guided when he or she asks to be led. The "knowing" does not come from knowledge but from "inner wisdom."

The powerful medicine people do not give their information away. Prophetic and healing talents are only given to those individuals who have proven that they have no interest in misusing them. Many of the talents of the medicine men and women were natural or earned powers that could not be taught to others. Secrets that could be shared were given to select people with the right character and dedication for years of study. As the old saying goes, when the pupil is ready the teacher appears.

The great ancient secret wisdoms come to those who work on their character first. The knowing is acquired when one has lifted one's self to a high enough plane to receive it. Few secrets exist on these higher planes of existence and little appears to happen by chance. Sometimes one needs a way to begin a quest for increased knowledge and self healing and discovery. My hope is that this book will help you begin that journey. Ho!

—Mary Dean Atwood, Ph.D.

Chapter One

Bushyhead, a medicine man, sat quietly among the shimmering aspen trees high above the snake-shaped canyon hundreds of feet below. As he sat, he felt the power of the location, where energies from the earth's magnetic field converged. The power was so great that at times the vibrations made him feel dizzy. All around the old man were huge clusters of wintering monarch butterflies, which clung to the towering eucalyptus trees. The very ground seemed to radiate electricity.

The eyes of the old Indian watched as two monarch butterflies prepared to mate. The male butterfly hovered by a eucalyptus blossom and caught the unsuspecting female lured there by the fragrant aroma. He grabbed her in the air and, after an airy, acrobatic routine, they fell to the ground where they mated. After mating, the male took off in flight with the female still dangling beneath him. But he had fulfilled his biological duty and slowly began to decompose, unable to continue the migration path of his mate. Her flight pattern dominated his as he struggled to pull loose from her. They were still connected by his already decaying appendage. That part of him, still embedded in the female as she twisted, turned their act of love into a dance of death. He fluttered helplessly to the ground, his fate sealed. Bushyhead watched as the male's legs finally stopped struggling. The dying butterfly carefully folded his wings before the final moment, ending his life with poise and dignity. And the female continued her trek north to lay her eggs under the leaf of a milkweed plant, to provide a source of food for her hatchling young.

This event synchronized with Bushyhead's purpose for coming to this location, a fact that did not surprise the old shaman. Life and death cycles were on the old Indian's mind today. The events of such a person's life often attracted occurrences in nature that foreshadowed his or her own.

Bushyhead made sure that he did not get too close to the edge of the canyon as he closed his eyes in meditation. The pull of Mother Earth's magnetic fields, called ley lines, might draw him unwittingly over the edge if he leaned too far over. He was not ready to join the Grandfathers yet, and when they did beckon, he planned to choose the time and place himself. Besides, like the butterfly, he had duties to perform before he left for his ancestral home in the sky.

This was his favorite spot to communicate with the Great Spirits for divination and guidance. He knew that the spectacular, ridged canyon cast a special spell even before he received his first spirit visit here. As a child, he used to pass by it as he followed the hunters on their quests for game. During one expedition, he had clearly heard someone beckoning him to visit. He had desperately wanted to explore the enticing area but considered it disrespectful to wander off from the others.

Bushyhead wasn't known in his village for his tracking abilities or for his skilled use of a bow and arrow. His father knew him to be less than gifted as a hunter, but rarely embarrassed him by saying so openly. The shaman thought then that perhaps his parents sensed other destinies for him. But now, remembering their permissiveness, he knew that they had acted in the typical Indian way. Like other Indian children, he was never punished physically.

Once he had lied to his mother, telling her that he followed the hunters who left early that morning. It took him all day to trek to his mysterious mountain and, when he returned home, everyone was asleep, including the hunters. Nothing was said because the tribe members simply thought that he didn't track well enough to follow! By then, however, Bushyhead had become too fascinated with the feelings of his special place to care. Whenever he visited the area, an undefined yearning overpowered him. The unseen and the unknown called out. Long before he left on his vision quest (a puberty rite) in the wilderness, he knew exactly where he would go.

During one winter visit, the young Indian's eye was caught by sparkles between the frothy snow-covered pine branches. He did not know then that these were the visible signs of nature sprites. But, as his powers of special sight developed, he would watch them play and interact with each other, their bodies transparent against the landscape they served. Bushyhead's favorite spirit was an old, withered earth gnome. This gnome was the leader of the area's earth sprites, whose task it was to oversee the evolution of the animals dwelling below the earth. Bushyhead chuckled the day he recognized the reason for his favoritism—he and the crusty old gnome shared similar characteristics and spiritual duties.

Today, Bushyhead had come to receive information from the spirit world about an important issue for his tribe. He was getting on in years, and probably no more than fifty moons remained for him. Death itself no longer frightened him because he knew of his future in the Path of Souls. His main concern centered around the selection of the medicine person that would take his place and care for the living after he was gone. Like the butterfly, he, too, wanted to contribute to the future before death came.

It was common practice for a gifted child or relative of a medicine person to inherit the position. Such a person usually displayed certain traits, even as a child, that indicated his or her future as a shaman. Some had prophetic dreams or spirit visitations. Others had visions during illnesses that foretold a possible fate of the tribe or proclaimed needed leadership. For example, Bushyhead's old mentor, Yellow Hawk, appeared to die and then come back to life, indicating special purpose and honor; and a male cousin, Flower Fox, had chosen women's ways instead of men's and showed special talent for setting and healing bones.

Bushyhead's sister had married into a clan with Comanche ancestry. They believed that those who slept bravely on the grave of a Comanche medicine man would inherit his power. Although Bushyhead doubted that such a transfer of power occurred, he assured himself that the ghost of a Comanche shaman would make sure that a person earned his or her power through bravery, or take the person's soul!

Most members of the tribe thought that all you needed to do was will your power to someone. But Bushyhead knew that the special person was selected by the Great Spirit to help the tribe. Once chosen, the person then faced years of demonstrated dedication before he or she could receive the sacred power. Sincerity of purpose, integrity, and honor dis-

19

played by the chosen one meant safety for the tribe. None of Bushyhead's sons and daughters had shown the necessary qualities, so no training ever began for them.

At first, he thought that his favorite daughter, Wounded Deer, would follow in his footsteps, but she proved too fragile. She bled to death during the birth of her only child, Little Hummingbird. Her passing saddened Bushyhead more than anything else he had experienced. For a while, it seriously threatened his belief in the ancestors and damaged his confidence in himself and his beloved spirits.

Pangs of guilt mixed with pains of loss overtook Bushyhead at her memory. He experienced numerous regrets throughout his lifetime, but his failure to save his daughter stung him like a hundred hornets. If only he had used the right herb or asked the proper spirit for guidance, she would be alive today. But he had failed to meditate long enough to get the proper guidance. He had known that she was fragile, but Bushyhead was totally unprepared for her sudden death.

Her passing did not prevent him from loving his small, round-faced granddaughter, however. Little Hummingbird intrigued him because of her way with animals. Birds flocked around her. She had a special essence that attracted them. Because of this, Bushyhead suspected that the death of his daughter had foretold the birth of a future healer. Perhaps the spirits had acted for a reason and he had done nothing wrong after all. He relaxed with that thought. Still, he feared that Little Hummingbird was too young to learn the sacred ways, and Bushyhead knew that there was little time left before he left for the world of the ancestors.

If no one took the shaman's place, the knowledge given him by the spirits would be lost forever. The wrong person could never be given the old ways of wisdom. With no one to inherit the position of healer, the tribe suffered deeply. Often, it was some time before someone claimed the position and began to prove him or herself through demonstrations of power. If the new shaman was power hungry or dishonest many more problems could develop in the tribe.

Bushyhead remembered Coyote Tooth, a bone healer in the tribe, and his inept attempts to take Bushyhead's position as tribal medicine man. What would he try after Bushyhead was gone? The old man's mind clouded when asked to dwell on this evil witch. The shaman knew that his power far exceeded that of Coyote Tooth, but rational thoughts and decisions concerning this old crone seemed to ball up and become fuzzy, like clumps of clouds over a summer meadow. It especially angered Bushyhead that Coyote Tooth pretended senility in his presence, but tried to convince others of his powerful medicine—particularly the children. The spirits warned Bushyhead of witchcraft designed to dethrone him, but old Coyote Tooth's power proved useless against the shaman's higher spiritual forces.

A few incidents when his own power had lessened stuck in Bushyhead's memory. But this time he saw that there was a pattern. When Bushyhead had acted too proudly or wanted to show off his skills or became too emotionally involved, Coyote Tooth's magic had gained an edge. *"Why had he not thought of this connection before!"* Well, being humble before the spirits and staying objective and unemotional from now on would take care of that problem.

Anyway teaching a new healer would take care of any future challenges from Coyote Tooth. That issue decided upon, Bushyhead went on to the reason for his current pilgrimage to his place of mystical wonder—the identification of his successor through divination and communion with his guardian angels.

Bushyhead arose with the sun and began to pray to his spirit guardians and asked for help in identifying his future pupil. He could see the purple light undulating behind closed eyelids and knew that the spirits were present. He then began his dialogue with his council of guardian angels, whom he had talked with many times before. Each being had a distinct personality, Bushyhead saw them all clearly. One was dressed as a Grandfather in a buckskin and had antlers on his head. Another, a woman, wore a robe of a white buffalo skin. Several of his guides wore long flowing robes with huge wings projecting behind them. One was a beautiful woman with long black braids. She wore a golden belt around her waist. A purple plume fluttered from the belt. One angel teacher, glowing with light and wearing an iridescent robe, moved his great white wings and spoke.

"Bushyhead, you are an honorable spiritual man and the council is pleased to continue its help whenever you are in need. We have been waiting for you to ask us for guidance with this situation. You will find the answer in a rock located by your medicine bag, but you already know the answer. Trust yourself. Let the truth be revealed to you even though it is painful. We will help you, our brother, as you continue on your path of many lessons on Earth."

Rising from his prayer and somewhat shaken from his trance state, Bushyhead walked slowly toward his medicine bag. The wind gusted around him in a whirlwind, scattering leaves, which clothed his body in a temporary wreath. As he approached the tree that held his medicine bag, a gleam of sunlight sparkled on the ground and illuminated a crystal fragment embedded in a rock. It was triangular in shape, much like the skull of a dog or coyote.

He sat down with his back to the tree, gathering strength from its emanations, and began to turn the rock over in his hands. Choosing one side, he stared with slightly unfocused eyes at the rock. Immediately, he saw in the lower section of the rock an irregular reddish band or stain. In it, to the left, was a darker figure that resembled a medium-sized, hunched-over animal with its tail between its legs. The stained area began to make him think of blood. *"Oh*, he thought, *I am supposed to be divining new visions, and instead I return to visions of death and blood."*

To the far right in the stain, a vertical band of crystal appeared in the shape of an angel or ghost clothed in a long robe. At the top, an eagle feather and a birdlike spirit floated in midair. A circle on the ground encompassed the figures. To the right of the stained area, lay a small, white figure. "Oh Spirits," cried Bushyhead, "I ask for an answer and I get nothing but a medicine wheel with a bird spirit in the air and an animal hunched over a figure stained with red."

At this moment, Bushyhead jerked back and wailed as though he was a wounded bear in unbearable agony from an arrow shot between its shoulder blades. He had realized the meaning of his vision and the discovery rendered him helpless. He gasped for breath as his chest began to stop rising and falling.

The back of his neck chilled as memories of the night his beloved daughter died raced to consciousness. His head ached as if it had been overstuffed with heavy matting as he

22

struggled to remember. In the corner of his mind, he could see a shadow entering the birthing place where his feverish daughter lay in childbirth. At the time, he ignored everything but the care of his daughter, Wounded Deer, for he knew that her condition was perilous. He sat in a trance trying desperately to think of the proper prayer to offer. At that moment he heard an owl hoot outside in a tree and his blood froze with fear—Wounded Deer would die and there was nothing that he could do. Soon the painful contractions of labor forced the birth of the baby.

He reached for the mixed herbal brew that sat in the shadows to his left. He held it to her lips and after she drank it, blood began to flow uncontrollably from her body. The drink was supposed to be an herb to stop the flow of blood. Instead, it had turned into a blood thinner! The mixture had been altered by someone in the darkness. His daughter had been murdered so that she could not inherit the position of medicine woman. His head pounded with rage at himself for his blindness and against the enemy, who had defeated him when he was at his weakest.

Bushyhead fell on his knees and thanked the guardian spirits for allowing him to remember this incident. The tiny figure that lay beside the ghostly spirit of his beloved daughter was his granddaughter, Little Hummingbird, who was to be the future medicine woman for his people. However, Bushyhead knew that he could not disclose this information because her enemy, Coyote Tooth, would kill her, as well. Bushyhead decided that he would train her in secret. Once she had acquired his power, she would be safe from Coyote Tooth's magic.

TALKING TO YOUR GUARDIAN ANGEL

There are reports from people all over the world who have seen a saint or spirit, depending upon each person's religious framework. Spirits and angels change into the form offering the most comfort and help to those in need. The Great Spirit, the Grandfathers and Grandmothers, the Thunderbeings, the Sun, and other nature or animal deities (interchangeable in their form with humans) were the spirit forms that Native Americans conceptualized as the highest angels. These powerful spirits were more accessible to spiritual leaders but they listened to prayers made by everyone. The lesser spirits, which were available for everyday help or for practical matters, appeared more often in animal form, but occasionally they came as nature or plant beings.

Everyone today has an angel or spirit guide who will come to his or her aid, if asked. Talking with your guide enables you to ask for solutions to problems and reach better decisions. It is easier than you might imagine to communicate with these heavenly helpers. You may be able to converse the first time you try, but others will need a little practice and perseverance before communication occurs. Just keep in mind, if you desire it, it will happen. Try the following exercise before reading on.

Always choose a time when you are alone to do your meditation. Burn sage or another smudge and a candle to help attract the angels as well as to clear the room of interfering vibrations. The room should be darkened when you are first learning to concentrate. Eliminate music, ringing phones, and other interruptions.

You should have a strong desire to talk with your guardian angel. If you are totally sincere in your efforts, it will happen. While concentrating, take in three slow deep breaths through your nose and let them out through your mouth. Now energetically clap your hands three times. Close your eyes. Concentrate on looking up toward the center of your forehead with both eyes rolled upward and inward. This is the location of your third eye. Keeping your eyes closed, concentrate on the color that you see before you. The color may or may not be brilliant and it may fade at the edges, so try to define the color as closely as you can. Remember the color.

Repeat the entire exercise in full. If you see the same color, repeat the breathing and the clapping several times, noting any change in color. Do not read the following paragraphs until you have done this exercise.

Color Analysis

Purple   Crown energy center and the desired color for communication with the highest spirit guides.

Indigo (dark, red-tinted blue)   Third eye energy center through which you may intuit messages from your guides or at least your higher self.

Blue   Throat energy center used to receive messages from your self or higher self. This is the location of the mental/energy center where thoughts originate.

Yellow   Heart energy center where higher feelings such as love and devotion originate. Attachments, attractions, and yearnings also derive from this center.

Green   Solar plexus center is a person's power base. Here the personality exerts will and self-control. Emotion often rules. Fear, jealousy, and anger originate from this center.

Red or Orange Red   Root center operating on a physical level, concerned with basic safety and physiological needs.

The goal is to perceive a purple color in your mind's eye. The purple is a signal you are at a high enough vibratory level (spiritually speaking) to be able to communicate with your spirit helpers.

For most people it is necessary to practice before they can envision purplish hues. Those seeing blue, indigo, or similar shades find they soon can raise the level to purple during meditation, with practice. Some people start out in the blue and then raise their color level during their spiritual conference.

People seeing yellow are on a higher emotional plane but must raise their consciousness to a mental/spiritual level for communication with their guides or higher self. It is fairly easy for those individuals on this level to begin to see blue or purple.

A predominant green color may indicate either an obsession with loss of control or fear. If you see this color, then emotional concerns of everyday living are interfering with your higher spiritual development and communication. One of the most common reasons for this is that you were not in a relaxed enough state when you started.

People who continue to see only red or orange after repeated practice will need other measures to achieve the higher colors. Prayer, meditation, reading of spiritual literature, or change in routine is sometimes necessary. Sometimes it helps to ponder current security fears or passions that tend to keep the individual at the root level. Patience and practice may be required to shift the consciousness toward higher levels.

Occasionally, a person will see black. This may mean a problem with visualizing, which can be helped by trying to smell, feel, or taste the color purple. Sometimes black means that a person is ready to drop off to sleep. If you are one of those people who go to sleep instantly when you go to bed, you should meditate upright in a sitting position.

Those people having trouble with color visualization need not despair. Anxiety and obsession, which sometimes get in the way, can be overcome by achieving a light trance state before you attempt to talk to your angelic hosts. Use a guided imagery tape, celestial music, relaxation exercise, or self-hypnosis. Precede this with a hot bath or sauna. It will also help if you give up unhealthy foods and alcohol.

At this point, do not worry about achieving the color purple in your mind's eye. It will appear later. Use this only as a measure of progress toward verification of spiritual levels.

After practicing to obtain the highest level color possible (regardless of what color it is), you are ready to begin talking to your spirit guide. Sometimes, intense desire and knowing that you will be able to talk with your guides will catapult you into that vibratory level. Below is a sample of a conversation designed to bring your guides to you. You do not have to use these exact words; you may use your own. The words of the dialogue are not as important as the sincerity of intentions. However, it is essential that you have your purpose for the discussion clearly in mind before you begin.

Dialogue

"Hello, my spiritual friends and advisors, the Grandmothers and the Grandfathers. Thank you for coming to talk with me today. I know I have guardian angels who watch over me. I appreciate your help and want you to know I desire your assistance at all times. I want to become a more spiritual person. I ask you to surround me with white light so that I can attract the highest spirit helpers. I would like to talk with my highest angel available.

I ask you now for guidance. I need counsel and advice. The one decision (problem, happening, situation) is _____ . What do you advise?"

Begin by letting your own higher self answer your question if you do not "hear or know an answer." Continue to talk and keep the dialogue flowing. When your spirit guides speak, you will know, because the colors behind your closed eyes will begin to change and flutter. The predominant colors should be purples and blues with some silver, gold, or flashes of white light. Do not focus on this process deliberately, because it will disappear as you switch to your left brain analysis. When you find that you are seeing another color, such as yellow, red, orange, or green, you will know that you have taken over the conversation. Relax, take three breaths, intensely desire your guide, clap your hands three times, and begin again. For those persons who are stuck in lower colors, continue your conversation and sincerity of intent and your angels will aid you every way they can, both in your problem and in enabling you to eventually see the purplish hues.

Answers coming from ourselves can occasionally slip in. This usually occurs when we are thinking of highly emotional issues and of answers that we want to hear. An important decision with suspected ego involvement should be checked out again before acting on the information received. The colors seen will help you decide. Of course, you will know that later when the answers that you received are shown to be incorrect. You are most likely to hear the wrong answers when intense desires intervene or when events affecting your self-esteem or pride are involved.

More often than not, however, you will find yourself amazed with the clarity, depth, and accuracy of the information that you receive. It may be hard to remember all that was said when you emerge from your higher state of being. You will, however, remember the most important solutions and aspects of your questions.

You will eventually develop a "feel" for answers coming from your guides. For example, they will use a different way of talking than you use. They always use the pronoun *we*. They may refer to you in endearing terms or be humorous. Sometimes you will receive information from them that you do not want to hear. Information may be new to you or unexpected. They present messages in the best way for you to learn from them. The angels are experts in metaphors and N.L.P. (neurolinguistic programming).

They may use a word that you do not know or give you an answer technically beyond your skills or vocabulary. Sometimes, it is necessary to stop the conversation in order to write down words or messages, because when you communicate with your guides, you go into a deep meditative state, bypassing the detailed memory part of the left brain.

Your spirit guides eagerly give help when you use intensity in requesting an answer. Emotion gives power, provided that you do not have an emotional investment in hearing a certain answer. In addition, motivation is important. Your angels will be most eager to help when you are trying to aid other people or work out problems for the good of all.

Your guardian angels wait for your communication. They want to help you improve your life and will accept the challenge eagerly. Your angel spirits have only love for you just as you are. But, they always work for the highest aims and will never hurt anyone else in the process. To help facilitate the communication with your guides, always be as clear and precise as possible with your request or situation. Specifically, what is your question? What do you need to know? Set out to deal with only one question or issue during each meditation.

Rock Divination

The ideal rocks for divination should be between the size of an orange and a basketball. If they get too heavy, you cannot turn them over to use the other side (however, one side will suffice in some cases). Let your intuition guide you when selecting your stone. Ideally, you want to be in a location with numerous choices where you can walk around and select a stone at random. Before you pick up your rock, decide on the question that you want answered. Keep this issue firmly in your mind as you select your stone. When you see one that feels right, take it to your place of meditation or, if the rock is large, sit down beside it. Always return your rock to its original location when finished as it may be there for a reason.

In silence, meditate softly to your spirit guides and ask for guidance and vision. Relax your body and clear your mind of all thoughts. Use the method most effective for putting yourself in a meditative state. Remind yourself of the question to be divined. Take the rock and turn it around until one side appeals to you. Clear your mind now of all thought and focus on the pictures you see in the rock. Let your mind flow naturally. Without evaluating your pictures, state them one at a time as you see them. Beginners should write down their images or briefly draw them. Take your time and be creative in the process. After you have finished writing down all the pictures you have seen, turn the rock over to another side and begin again.

After you have derived at least ten pictures, state the original question you are divining to yourself and apply the question to each of the ten pictures. What could the picture indicate for the question? How does it apply? Is there a common connection between the images? Where is there a possible answer? Let your mind weave a solution from the pictures. All information may not apply in an obvious way, but delve deeply into hidden possibilities or solutions. Let your mind "free associate" (say aloud your thoughts to each picture without direction or censorship). Sometimes, the answer becomes obvious with several pictures. At other times, all of the pieces of the puzzle must be analyzed together before a solution appears. What was the answer to your question?

Chapter Two

Little Hummingbird shuffled along the well-travelled path, kicking up dust as she walked. Looking back, she noticed that her beaded moccasins left footprints in the soft trail used by villagers going to the river. At this point, the trail was wide and well worn by tribal members going east. Beyond the river, the mountain range skirted the valley, guarding Pumpkin Vine Village from outsiders. Here the main trail split into a multitude of smaller arteries, weaving snakelike patterns up and around the mountain.

The terrain was mostly prairie, but there were several groupings of small aspens scattered among rocky ridges and tall grasses. Higher up the mountain, the trees became taller and thicker and the terrain rockier, the prairie eventually ceasing to exist.

After Little Hummingbird crossed the huge felled tree that served as a bridge across the shallow river, she turned sharply left and ascended a little-used trail toward the coldest and darkest side of the mountain.

She wanted to locate the bushes with the red berries that she had discovered several weeks ago while exploring the area with a friend. She had stuck some of the berries into her gathering basket and her aunt had found them. "Oh, little daughter, get me more and I will use them when I make your next pair of moccasins. These berries make the most brilliant red dye, but they are hard to find."

Little Hummingbird could just imagine the delighted look on her aunt's face when she presented her with the fruit.

The young Indian loved the feeling of walking through the woods. A powerful feeling came over her that she was majestic and wise, like the tree spirits. She remembered the previous fall when she had taken this path. The leaves had been glorious, bathed in red and yellow. They had dropped off the trees and whirled and cascaded down around her while the sun peeped through them, showering her with gold and orange.

She also remembered the feeling of estrangement that engulfed her as she watched the leaves fall. Though she felt omnipotent and glorified in the beauty bestowed by Mother Earth, an incredible feeling of loneliness gripped her. It was as if she knew more than her young mind could possibly remember. Feelings emerged in her that had no memories with them, as if they had been experienced in another time and place. Her grandfather had said her spirit lived before, but his words meant little until then.

Little Hummingbird remembered watching her grandfather leave for his pilgrimage several moons before. His body was stooped and he did not take time to talk with her as was his custom. She loved her grandfather more than anyone and thought him the wisest man in the whole world. She worried about him, for she knew he was getting old and had many responsibilities for the tribe.

Perhaps her empty feeling had something to do with her mother, whom she never knew. Surely she would have been punished with dreadful happenings if she had caused her mother's death. Her Aunt Morning Star described her mother as small with tiny hands and feet. Her eyes had been big and beautiful and her face shone with beauty and innocence, so her mother had been named Wounded Deer.

Somehow, Little Hummingbird felt she must be ugly by comparison, but her grandfather had assured her that she simply looked different. She had the same inner glow, the same look of innocence, and the same big dark eyes, but on a rounder face. Bushyhead said she reflected everything that was good in her mother without the physical weakness. Little Hummingbird grew healthy and strong. The spirits told him she would live to be old and would have no trouble during childbirth.

Her reflection in the lake revealed the truth in his words. Wondering if the Great Spirit would consider it wrong to be satisfied with the way you looked, she nevertheless liked what she saw in the water. Maybe others did too, for she collected stares from them as well. The glances used to make her uneasy, because she did not feel comfortable receiving attention. When men from her tribe had stared, it had given her a bad feeling and she had found an excuse to leave their presence. Coyote Tooth glanced frequently, and she believed that he had talked about her to his son, Grey Badger.

Then one day not long ago, she found herself wanting Grey Badger to look at her! She felt a strange need to return his glances, and when their eyes joined, she felt a force pull her toward him as if they should always be together. He was handsome, and had none of the shifty features or devious ways of his father. Grey Badger, now sixteen years old to her eleven, was as big as any man. Embarrassed to ask her grandfather about Grey Badger, she thought of a way to talk about him with Aunt Morning Star. She planned to ask her about several other people at the same time so that her aunt would not suspect her interest in Grey Badger.

Little Hummingbird continued up the dusty trail, hating to get her new moccasins dirty. She wanted to keep them pretty and clean, the way they were before she wore them. They were covered with beads, so it was only the soles that got soiled. Her aunt had worked many hours sewing the beads. This was the sixth pair that her aunt had made for her. Her first pair had stayed clean because she had been an infant at the time and could not walk. She had spent most of her time in a cradle board. She still had the tiny shoes. She also had her umbilical cord stored in a beaded buckskin pouch for good luck and prosperity.

She could imagine the intricate red designs and beads her aunt would sew on her shoes. She had little interest in the crafts traditionally used by the women, and her aunt said that she took after her grandfather, who shunned men's interest in the hunt. "I hope you become a medicine woman because you will not be skilled at weaving or sewing," Aunt Morning Star used to say with a laugh. "As long as you have me here, I will do those things for you and when I join the spirits, maybe your daughter will make your moccasins."

Little Hummingbird continued her climb up the mountain. The path was narrow now, seldom used by anyone because it led to a dead end. Eventually, one could go no further as the trail ended in a high area with steep rocks. The area was quite safe for anyone in the tribe. The other side of the mountain, on which the neighboring tribe liked to hunt was off limits. She quickly dropped the thought of that area, remembering that her grandfather was much further beyond the village than she was. Before he left, he had told her of his power place, which he promised to show her someday. His power would protect them when they traveled, he had promised.

As she walked, she noticed an orange and black butterfly sunning itself on a poplar tree leaf. At first she thought it a monarch, but when she looked closer she saw it was a viceroy, which was smaller and a native to the area. It mimics the appearance of the monarch, which is poisonous and bad tasting, to protect itself from predators. Although it is nourishing and tasty, birds avoid it because of its markings.

As the climb steepened, she noticed a hummingbird darting in and out of the honeysuckle bushes to her right. Its tiny slender beak pulled nectar from the trumpet-shaped orange blossoms. Because she was named after the hummingbird that flew into the tepee after her birth, she paid particular attention to its activities.

Of course, birds and animals had been appearing to her since she was a toddler and she loved to talk to them. Their thoughts seemed to come to her as if she knew what they were thinking. If she was in a group of people, animals always singled her out. When she was younger, the larger ones darted at her so eagerly that she'd often topple over. Relatives and friends didn't listen when she tried to share her animal experiences with them. Again, her grandfather seemed to be the only one who understood.

The hummingbird began to fly in front of her as she walked. Occasionally, it turned around and flew backwards, its little tail twitching up and down as if waiting to see if she followed. When they arrived at the place where she wanted to collect the berries, Little Hummingbird veered off onto another path. Her tiny hummingbird friend swirled back several times, paused, turned to look at her, and flicked its tail. But, when she continued the other way, it flew on.

She felt sorry to see her bird friend leave, but knew that she had to return with a basket of berries. As she proceeded up the new path, the foliage thickened and the forest suddenly seemed darker. She hoped that she could remember where she had seen the berry bushes. As she searched, she remembered a previous animal experience.

She recalled the time when she was five years old and her

grandmother came to tell her of the tragic death of her pet raccoon, Friendly Eyes. Because he was a pet, he had no fear of people or animals around the camp. A rattlesnake, disturbed by a friendly poke from the raccoon's sharp claws, struck and killed the raccoon. Distraught, Little Hummingbird cried. This was the first time she remembered feeling that her heart would break in two. She threw herself on the ground and wailed. She had once seen a woman cut a piece of skin from her arm to honor the bravery of her dead warrior and she considered cutting herself with a rock in honor of Friendly Eyes.

Then a movement in a tree caught her eye. When she was able to catch her breath, she wiped the tears from her eyes, looked toward the tree, and then wiped them again to make sure that she saw correctly. There was Friendly Eyes, his little, fat striped body swaying back and forth as he climbed the tree. She laughed and started to run to her grandmother to tell her the good news.

She had hardly thought of this when grandmother walked up carrying Friendly Eyes, who was cold and dead. Her grandfather came up and put his arms around her, and she grabbed him. He asked her to bless Friendly Eyes on his trip back to the Lowerworld. She said, "Oh Grandfather, I saw Friendly Eyes scamper up the tree before you brought this raccoon. This must be another, because I know my friend and he seemed happy to see me."

Grandfather looked toward his wife and she backed slowly away, as if on cue. "My child, what you saw was Friendly Eyes' second body. You see, upon death, the connection between the spirit and the physical body is severed and the spirit body is freed. Friendly Eyes is happy because he saw you and because he is still climbing trees. Soon, however, his guardian spirit will come for him and he will leave happily."

"Where does he go, Grandfather?" she asked. "Will I ever see him again?"

Bushyhead picked up his little granddaughter and sat her on a rock so that she would be closer to his quiet voice. "Friendly Eyes will accompany his guardian spirit back to the Lowerworld where he will wait for his next assignment, overseen by higher teachers. Then, he will come back to earth as another raccoon or as another animal, perhaps a dog or wolf. You see, he evolved and advanced through his love and service to you. Now he will be assigned a higher level of being.'' Bushyhead thought for a moment, and cast his eyes upward. ''I have a strong feeling you will be given a dog or wolf cub to raise in the near future and this cub will be Friendly Eyes in another body.''

A year later, tears had come to Little Hummingbird's eyes as she was presented with a fuzzy grey ball by Uncle Running Stream when he returned from a hunting trip. Her uncle had said that it was unusual for such a small wolf cub to appear at the river alone. Wolves, unlike many animals, share in the care of their young. Once weaned, if the mother is injured or killed, the father takes over the feeding and training of the young. However, no parent was in sight and the small fellow was so hungry and thin that Running Stream knew the pup was close to death. Because Little Hummingbird loved animals, her uncle gave the cub to her.

She named him Lonely One and came to love him almost as much as she loved her grandfather. She remembered her grandfather had told her that certain animals were attracted to certain people. He said that her sincerity and devotion attracted animals like wolves, which were loyal and dependable. Ordinarily, Lonely One accompanied her on her travels, but that morning her uncle had taken him hunting.

Little Hummingbird realized she had been daydreaming and awoke when the tiny bird she had seen earlier dove down right in front of her face! She found herself walking along a dark path with no idea where she was. Warnings of her daydreaming echoed in her ears. The sky darkened and clouds crossed the tops of the huge trees. Although it was still light, the moon, which had already risen, illuminated the dark clouds speeding in front of its round glowing form. A storm had brewed while she daydreamed!

The tiny wings of the bird fluttered so fast that she hardly could see them in the dwindling light. He came back, again and again. She soon realized that the bird wanted her to follow. She started toward the bird and instantly it proceeded to lead her across a rocky hill and down the side of the mountain. When she no longer could see, it returned, fanning its wings close to her face.

Again and again, she crisscrossed over rocks and around

trees, never looking at the steep precipice directly below. At one point, the bird flew over such a dangerous jumping point that she hesitated to follow. However, she had no choice but to trust her bird guide. Surely he was a spirit sent to save her. She took a deep breath, jumped without looking down, and grabbed a tree limb just as she began to slip downward. About that time the sun broke through the dark clouds, spraying the mountain with light. She felt relief and optimism surface as she recognized familiar landmarks in the distance that joined the strange new path.

Soon, they were on the trail that she had taken on her way up the mountain. With relief, she headed quickly down the path marked with her footprints just as raindrops started to fall. As she watched the raindrops splattering on the dusty trail, she was startled to find that large footprints, only several hours old, duplicated her path up the hill. A chill ran up her spine and the tiny hairs on her arms stood straight up. Did a man follow her up the trail? Why would he not be on the hunting trail off to the west? Did anyone have a reason to follow her or, worse, want to hurt her? Had her bird friend brought her down the mountain quickly for a reason?

Her innocent mind dismissed any danger to herself. No doubt someone had been looking for a beehive and had taken the same trail. Aunt Morning Star would understand about the storm on the mountain, and Little Hummingbird would promise to return as soon as possible. Only this time, she would be sure to bring Lonely One to guide her home. As her tiny friend swerved high in the sky, Little Hummingbird thanked her bird spirit for the help.

ANIMAL SPIRIT COMMUNICATION

Developing communication with animal and bird spirits takes time, dedication, and patience. New attitudes and behaviors are required and there are no definite ways to assess your progress. Many experiences cannot be defined or put into categories. You must develop your intuition and perceptions as you gain experience in order to help you interpret events. Beginning to develop skills of communication with bird and animal spirits is an ongoing lifetime process with no definite answers.

Certain attitudes are needed to help you gain the attention and cooperation of your animal spirit friends. You will have to adapt four behaviors before beginning such communication, however.

1. Love and reverence for all living things.

2. Sincerity of motive and higher purpose.

3. Intense desire for spirit communication.

4. Follow a program to attract and help the bird and animal kingdom.

Respect for all living things and for the ways that they are connected is essential to attracting animals and animal spirits. This includes a knowledge of your own existence as a divine being. You must be aware of and appreciate the sacredness of nature and all her plants and creatures. This understanding is a prerequisite to any meaningful animal communication.

You, no doubt, already have this quality because you are reading this book. This quality is a feeling of love and empathy for all living things which is demonstrated when you attend an animal in distress, nurture a plant or pet, or take interest in the preservation and survival of animal and plant species on our planet.

The most important requirement is sincerity of motive and high spiritual purpose. Motive is everything. The same behavior with varying motives will bring completely different results. Always entertain the highest aims for all concerned in your goals and experiences in life. You can help obtain this difficult attribute by eliminating all doubts, fears, and angers from your thinking. Think positively and always for the good of all. Time is required to bring you to this ideal state of mind. Patience is necessary to change thought patterns and to receive help from the spiritual dimension because linear time does not exist on that plane.

The higher level animal and bird spirits are attracted to your appreciation and interest. Your intense desire acts as a powerful beam radiating outward into your environment. Wish for them and they will come to you. Spend time outside observing nature to help increase both the intensity of your desire and the spirits' availability. Living in the city makes it somewhat more difficult to have your friends visit, but they will find you anyway.

The fourth requirement for attracting your spirit helpers is to be helpful to them. The Native Americans were cognizant of this reciprocal interaction. They left small offerings of food or charms to be helpful to their spirit and animal helpers. Expand your appreciation of nature to include service and action, and they will come to you in gratitude.

Attracting Bird and Animal Spirit Helpers

1. Spend some time outdoors taking in the essence of nature, every day when possible. Walk around a park or the countryside. In inclement weather, drive around and park in a scenic location. Always do this alone so you can begin to sense what nature has to offer. This must be done in silence and solitude. When not possible, gaze out of an open window and focus on plants, trees, and birds. You will be amazed at what you can see outside your window.

2. Buy a bird feeder and position it to be seen when you look outside. Include some food for other animals on the ground.

3. Plant trees and shrubs that attract birds and animals. For example, a female pyracantha bush will attract a mockingbird as a permanent resident, which will give you many delightful moments.

4. If you want a pet, adopt either an animal at the pound or one being given away in the newspaper. Do not set out to buy a pedigreed animal or buy one impulsively in a pet store. However, if an opportunity for any pet comes along and it feels right, take it, because it may be a special friend.

5. Avoid the purchase of any product or chemical that is tested on animals. Buy natural cosmetics and toiletries that specify no animal testing. The best policy is to avoid purchasing most

chemicals, poisons, drugs, insecticides, commercial fertilizers, herbicides, pesticides, and all possible environmental pollutants.

6. Subscribe to a magazine that promotes animal welfare or ecology. Join an organization that is lobbying or working toward the improvement of conditions for animals, animal rights, or animal and plant habitats.

7. Volunteer to help at the zoo or with groups that preserve wildlife, or join "living" organizations that provide alternatives to euthanasia.

8. Avoid the use of plastics and styrofoam, as they are non-biodegradable and endanger the environment. Recycle paper and buy recycled goods.

9. Avoid products that use fluorocarbon propellants, which damage the ozone layer of the earth's atmosphere.

10. Eat foods that require lower amounts of energy to be produced, such as grains and vegetables. Animal products require a great deal of energy in their production.

Basically, any action taken by you to preserve or care for nature and her inhabitants will increase your spiritual consciousness and bring you many blessings. This new ecological awareness and action will send messages to the animal and bird spirits and tell them that you are ready to receive their assistance. Any task you take to protect your animal friends will be rewarded many times over. They will be attracted to you and begin to give you many rich experiences. The more interest and concern you show for them, the more help they will give you.

Animal Interpretation

Animal spirits communicate with us in many different ways and it is not always possible to distinguish among them. Ordinary animals, insects, and birds may be drawn to you by a vibration field surrounding your body. Song birds are drawn to yards with good vibrations. A friendly neighborhood dog will give you feedback about the warmth of your personality. Bumblebees or angry dogs give you different information. Basically, when insects, birds, or animals are around, they reflect the conditions present in your environment. These animals are not in spirit form, but they are sensitive to your magnetic field and are drawn to you for a reason. Use them as a barometer to assess yourself and your current environmental conditions.

Birds and animals from different dimensions or in spiritual forms may give you warnings or assistance. For instance, crows, hawks, and owls portend the future and are valuable assistants. Of course, the number of birds involved and the activities in which they are engaged are important in the interpretation. A single crow approaching you in unusual fashion may be a warning of a disappointment or a betrayal. But a group of crows chatting merrily in your tree may give you a sign of a friendly gathering that you will join.

If a person in your family is sick, an owl may portend a long illness or his or her death. If you are starting a project, seeing an owl may signal changes ahead or be a warning of a difficult time ahead.

Higher teachers may appear as birds or animals and offer experiences or lessons that provide information or guidance. When this happens, they appear in a form that is acceptable to the person and will avoid arousing suspicion. For example, a bear would not appear to you in the city. Birds and dogs are the most common form of higher spirit intervention. However, these experiences are rare and will not happen until a person has achieved the status of an adept.

Native Americans made no attempt at grouping their spirits in hierarchical form except for the Great Spirits, who were seen as the highest form of intelligence.

The following birds and animals are listed with suggested messages only as a guideline for you. Most important is the context in which they are seen or heard. Notice the rarity of the animal and its description, the activity of the animal, the number of birds or animals involved, its condition, the location, and its proximity and interaction with you. After these considerations, messages are to be interpreted with the personal context of each individual and his or her life's situation.

ANIMAL	MESSAGE
crow/raven	portent
bluebird	happiness
chickadee	optimism
red bird/cardinal	beauty
quail	family
bat	macabre

hummingbird	joy
robin	balance
meadowlark	protective
hawk	opportunity
owl	diviner
blue jay	pushy
peacock	ostentatious
wild pheasant/turkey	quick
sparrows	ordinary
mockingbird	imitative
magpie	knowledge
roadrunner	traveler
pigeon on ground	inertia
pigeon in air	mission
chicken	foolish
turkey	forgetful
parrot	playful
heron	spiritual
lark	weather
pelican	saver
eagle	highest power
canary	joy
snow goose	fidelity
domestic goose	quarrelsome
wild duck	adventure
flamingo	grace
red-headed woodpecker	resourceful
ostrich	stubborn
dog	loyalty
cat	independent
goat	friendly
bighorn sheep	conqueror
domestic sheep	follower
cow	docile
wild horse	freedom
race horse	high strung
workhorse	plodding
pig	intelligence
bull/stallion	sexual energy
buffalo	strength
rabbit	gentle
skunk	defended

porcupine	protected
raccoon	enterprising
possum	avoidance
otter	playful
badger	aggressive
armadillo	defended
beaver	accomplishment
squirrel	resourceful
turtle/tortoise	old wisdom
llama	practical
camel	ornery
burro/donkey	helpful
mule	stubborn
elephant	old memory
elk	brave
moose	pride
antelope	action
lynx	psychic
deer	loveliness
bear	strength
mountain lion/cougar	leader
coyote	cunning
fox	wily
wolf	organizer
snake	challenger
lizard/toad	old wisdom
frog	sorcery
chameleon	adaptable
cricket	disharmony
cockroach	lowest
fly	parasitic
butterfly	friendly
spider	deceit
beetle	hidden knowing
mole	lack foresight
rat	survivalist
mouse	busy
whale	universal mind
porpoise/dolphin	teachers
shark	killer
sturgeon	dominant
sea gull	freedom

Animal Diary

- Make a list of all the animals, insects, and birds you have noticed over the last several months.

- List unusual animal and bird sightings and interpretation.

- List recurring sightings.

- List animals or birds reappearing during lifetime.

Exercises

- Write what animal you most resemble, physically and with regard to personality.

- What animal do you think you might have been in a former life?

- Draw the animal that each member of your family seems most like.

Chapter Three

The sun, which had been smothered in clouds all day, burst out in gold and pink swirls as it set, casting long shadows on the tall pines surrounding Bushyhead, who was perched on his favorite boulder overlooking the canyon. The orange and black monarch butterflies continued to swarm overhead. Bushyhead felt hypnotized looking up at the thousands of butterflies circling and fluttering to and from the eucalyptus trees, where they hung in clumps. Their angelic appearance belied by their insect composition and taste. Swarms of thousands often omitted a faint musk caused by their preference for highly odorous plants and wet nesting places.

A hungry blackbird dipped toward the butterflies but swerved at the last minute to avoid contact. A bird that tastes a monarch seldom makes the same mistake twice. The taste is bitter and toxic. By feeding on poisonous plants, the butterflies become filled with pungent chemicals. The butterflies mate and migrate in peace, their enemies stymied. Time is their only fatal enemy.

Also a race against time, Bushyhead mapped out a plan to outwit his enemy, Coyote Tooth. He would train his granddaughter in secret to give her his sacred knowledge and power before he disclosed her identity to the tribe. She would be protected by her own power and his as long as he lived. The medicine man realized that Coyote Tooth watched him and could guess his secret. He had done it before. This time, Bushyhead, forearmed and forewarned, would prevent his granddaughter's death with the power he had received from his guardian angels. He asked the Grandmothers and Grandfathers to send Little Hummingbird a special guardian spirit. He asked his spirit council and power animals to guide him in the success of his plan.

The confidence in his own renewed power, received from his spiritual helpers, put his mind temporarily at ease. His thoughts jumped back and forth in time from the past to the present, as they had done for the entire time he spent at his power place. Mainly he focused on the past, as is common with the old, who have more time behind than before.

He wondered why a person had to get close to death before realizing what was important in life. It is as if we were blind, only to have our sight restored when it was too late to use it. We die with some higher visions unfulfilled and the knowledge of what we could have done to accomplish them.

The memories of his life were stacked on one another like the layers of rock exposed in the canyon below, each of which represented eons of time. Awareness that his entire human life span seemed a thin part of top soil only worsened his feelings of ineptitude. But what of previous life experienced? At first, his spirit had been a mineral, and then a plant, before acquiring the powers of animal and man. Where in the canyon wall were these ancient periods of time represented? Thousands of years, maybe millions had passed during his evolution.

Yes, now he felt his immorality, and knew himself to be a true part of the essence of the living, breathing universe. He had to admit that the spirits had been good to him, for they offered Bushyhead promises of future tasks to make up for any duties missed in the past.

He remembered the first time the spirits came to him, here on this mountain. He was only fourteen when he received his vision to become a healer. He went on a solitary journey, miles into the hills and without food, water, or any clothing other than an animal skin. This was a necessary ritual to prove that he was a man and worthy of hunter or warrior status. When he returned, his destiny was changed.

He remembered the day well. Visions from the spirits come vividly and are easily remembered, unlike ordinary dreams or thoughts. His father, his uncle and predecessor, Yellow Hawk, and an older cousin had shared the sweat lodge that preceded his vision quest. Since then, all the others had gone to join the great Thunderbeings in the sky.

His mind drifted back. After the sweat lodge, there was a tribal feast. He ate all he could hold of deer, wild turnips, and honeycakes made with berries, buffalo fat, and cornmeal, before he left alone for the wilderness. His mother did not motion to him as he left but her wide eyes followed and he saw her face grow pale, then twitch. She would do nothing to make him more vulnerable, such as show her fear and concern. As he walked off, he remembered that his cousin had gone on his vision quest the year before and had never returned. Rumors circulated as to his fate. Some thought he wandered into a cave and never came out, because human bones were found the following winter by hunters seeking refuge.

Another story suggested that his cousin had been killed by a neighboring tribe in retaliation for the kidnapping of a woman by a member of his tribe. Everyone knew that one person's life would be taken as the Indian way of retaliation. Ordinarily the avengers would seek out a person older than his cousin, but he was tall and looked older than his age. If he had died in the cave alone, they still waited for the right person. Or, maybe two boys would equal one adult! To feel fear often invited trouble, so he quickly dismissed it.

The first day he felt excited, anxious, and vulnerable as he walked. He was unclothed but carried a deerskin. He wanted to sing and jump over logs and grab friendly branches. But he must proceed cautiously so that no member of an enemy tribe would spot him. He wanted to go south, which was the least likely area to encounter enemies, but instead he chose to go north to his place of power. Surely, the spirits would take notice of him now! He stood little chance against an armed enemy warrior so he hoped only for the possibility, not the reality.

The most important thing was to spend his nights in the location of the unseen and unknown power. The place was high on ridge with more likelihood of wind and rain, but again, he dismissed the negative aspects from his mind and recalled that the rules allowed him to scoop out a hole in the earth to make a little shelter. He arrived at dusk, and chose a place that was partly sheltered and hidden. Then, with a large stick and rock, he dug out a place in which to lie at night. He knew that in several days his senses would not be as keen.

He sprinkled sacred sage to the four directions and prayed to the upper and lower spirits. He laid out offerings of tobacco and corn to the spirits in the hope that they would be pleased and take notice of him. He took solace in the precious articles that his mother had given him from her medicine bundle—an eagle feather, a rock with power, a blue bead, and red willow, an herb to attract the spirit helpers. He was thankful for his animal skin cover as well.

He watched as large numbers of birds crisscrossed above him. Creatures had a way of sensing special events before they happened. But was it a favorable omen or an ominous one? He noted a hawk sitting off in the distance watching. He'd heard that medicine men or witches sometimes transformed themselves into animals, and he wondered if it could be Yellow Hawk in disguise. Some people became terrified at the prospect of a forthcoming spell or of death when they encountered the possibility, but he found that the thought comforted him. He knew Yellow Hawk was honorable.

He also felt safer at twilight, at which time a mockingbird sat above him in a tree and sang a beautiful song. This particular bird seemed to have been around him as far back as he could remember. Once, in a dream, the bird had appeared as a beautiful Indian woman clothed in the skin of the white buffalo. She told Bushyhead that she watched over him, but he feared ridicule so he told no one about it. He did get up enough nerve to mention the dream to Yellow Hawk, who laughed and patted him on the head. Later, the shaman teased him, saying the mockingbird knew how to read his thoughts. Bushyhead remembered that as a child his mother had told him that mockingbirds could understand human language.

He surprised himself by easily staying awake all night. He felt warm enough, or perhaps he was too excited to notice the cold. When morning came, he began to experience hunger pains, which grew worse as the day went on. To keep his mind off food, he explored the arroyo, preferring to stay on low ground. In the sandy canyon, he found human footprints that were at least three or four days old. He crept quietly, not wanting to attract any attention should anyone be around. He walked backward to leave tracks going in the opposite direction.

As the sun began to fade, he paid tribute to the Sun Father by placing his hands upward toward the orange-red sunset, looking himself like a giant bird perched for flight on the ridge. A huge group of migrating monarchs, recently arrived

47

from their summer home, fluttered about him and wrapped his naked body in a living cocoon of color, adding to the orange and bronze sky. Their wings brushed across his skin in feathery wisps, as if to dust him before an offering.

The second night, he felt cold, weak, and frightened. He feared that his spirit animal might not think him worthy of a gift of power. He would be humiliated if he returned with nothing but tales of hunger and woe. The appearance or sound of a power animal would indicate strength and special power for the rest of his life. But if he failed to attract a guardian animal, he would have to go through the ordeal all over again.

Surely, the spirits would feel sorry for him and come to his aid. He decided to cry out to let them know he suffered. Pain welled up inside him, more than he had felt before. The louder he cried, the more likely it was that the spirits would hear him, but he had to be careful. A neighboring warrior also might be listening to his lament!

Fatigue began to overtake him, and he struggled to fight sleep. He sat upright with his legs tucked under him to stay awake, pains shooting up his lower limbs and buttocks. Several times, he awoke as he was falling over, but soon the sun peeped over the horizon and he stood up.

Thirst became an obsession. He licked the dew from the leaves to keep his tongue from swelling. He found himself praying for rain to catch in his mouth. The sparkling stream from the river below beckoned him with taunting gurgles of cool, crystal water to soothe his parched throat. Memories of animals dying of thirst two years ago during the great drought haunted his brain. Villagers talked of failure to pay homage to the water spirits. A man who had thrown a vulture's carcass into the river, showing disrespect to the Water Babies, was banned forever from the tribe.

Half the time allotted for his quest was gone and nothing had happened to indicate a vision or message. He felt weak from hunger, and caught himself imagining roasted duck and his mother's stew of corn and acorns. Weariness from his sleepless vigil overwhelmed him, so he stayed close to his campsite and doubled over to preserve his body heat.

The third night, he was sick. Nausea overtook any temporary fears for his welfare. Dry heaves convulsed his empty stomach. He felt hot and several times he woke up drenched with sweat even though he also shivered with cold. The young Indian never had suffered like this before, and death surfaced in his mind as a welcome possibility.

Time passed too quickly, and he suspected that he had gone to sleep sitting up. The full moon illuminated the landscape, casting shadows over swaying trees and bushes. Hearing activity, he cautiously peered, through glazed eyes, toward a boulder on his right. Something moved in the shadows. His heart stopped, for it looked like someone walking on two legs, surely a warrior coming to kill him! As tall as a giant, the figure would kill him or take him back to torture! The shadow moved toward him. Startled, he realized that it was transparent. It was the ghostly image of a bear! The bear had the bushiest head he had ever seen. It was a giant male with huge paws and claws. Was it the ghost of a bear slain by his people, set for revenge, or was it his power animal come to give him a sign? He held his breath in fear as he waited for the answer.

The bear raised up over him as if to eat him alive. The Indian thought, "If I am to die, then I will not go down without a fight." He lunged at the bear only to fall through the image and tumble down over the large rock shelf precariously close to the edge of the ridge. Peeping out over the boulder, he tried to keep the rest of himself hidden. He saw the image of the bear lean over him, and then his mind faded into nothingness.

A sensation of floating brought him to awareness. He felt paralyzed, as if in a nightmare. He gradually began to rise in the air and observed the scene beneath from a position above the pine trees. The bear with the bushy head was sitting beside a fire accompanied by other strange animal and bird forms. He saw himself lying behind the rock. He heard loud noises and the screaming of humans in pain. His own throat gripped as if in a noiseless scream, but emitted no sound.

Suddenly, he felt safer as he realized that he could observe everything from a distance. The rest of his fear faded as he heard the strains of a song. The bear began to sing a song that soothed the other creatures with him. At least, the horrible wailing had ceased. The bear sang of the power in him, of how the power came to him, and of how it flowed from

49

him over to other people, thereby healing them. The young boy felt stronger, as if the words of the song surged through his body, and gave it strength. He, too, wanted to sing that song, and soon it flowed from his lips. Back on the ground, he tried to get up but fell over and started to float. Soon he floated back to his bed, guided by something. He felt fur brush his face and smelled burning sage and another appealing fragrance he could not identify. He heard and felt nothing else and soon left the world to sleep.

The next day, his vision quest completed, the young Indian walked back to Pumpkin Vine Village, which encircled a lake of clear, blue-green water. Smoke rose from the cooking fires and reminded him of food for the first time since his vision. He was surprised to find that many tribe members waited eagerly for his return. They had been told by the medicine man, Yellow Hawk, that an important vision had taken place that was of interest to the tribe. The girls his age took special pains to make sure he noticed them as he walked by, feeling self-conscious. He avoided their smiles and tried to ignore any feelings of pride that might jeopardize his power.

In the sweat lodge, he explained his vision to the elders. He would always remember their faces, their skin wrinkled and old like golden leather, gleaming with the resin of sage smoke. Yellow Hawk then told his dream of the bear who came from the great star spirits to give special power to his nephew, the next medicine man. The spirits had disclosed previous lifetimes that the youth had spent as seer and healer. His power animal, the bear, would guide him as would his other spirit helpers. Yellow Hawk would begin to train his young nephew, now named Bushyhead, at the next new moon.

Startled to find himself back in the present time, the old shaman awoke from his reverie and looked up as a mockingbird landed on the rock beside him. He reached over to pet the bird on the head. He never touched the animals in the presence of his people because the power frightened them. The old man now thought of Yellow Hawk, who had trained him in the sacred ways before he joined his ancestors in the Milky Way. Now he would have to return the favor to the tribe.

FINDING YOUR POWER PLACE

To find a location where you can sit and reflect or meditate, explore surrounding areas. Long distances may not be necessary. Neighborhood parks contain some surprising places for meditation. The key ingredient is foliage. You must have an area where you can have privacy without prying eyes or excess noise. If you are lucky, a spiritual energy or force will be present in your secluded spot. It may be necessary to travel further. National forests, lakes, river banks, and mountains all provide countless areas isolated enough for reflection and thought, often with powerful positive energies.

Finding true power centers or sacred locations is more difficult. Mountains act as antenna and certain points or crevices are funnels for magnetic fields. Mount Sinai, Machu Picchu, and the Himalayas are world renowned as strong, sacred energy centers. But pilgrimages to these areas are costly and difficult for westerners and are usually once-in-a-lifetime journeys.

Natural springs and caverns are frequently good sites for spiritual renewal. Energy from the earth emanates from these holes in the ground, drawing to them spirit life and human life alike. Waterfalls and hot springs are naturally cleansing because of the presence of ozone and negative ions in the air.

Trees also have positive energies, as do some natural rocks and plants. The pine and oak tree both vibrate on high spiritual frequencies. Trees are healers and to sit among them invites physical rejuvenation and spiritual renewal. To sit with your back to them or to hug them will facilitate healing in the body. Forests, such as those in the Great Rocky Mountains, are popular locations for quests and for exploring.

Boulders also have desirable magnetic qualities. This is why locations such as the Garden of the Gods in Colorado Springs attract thousands of people a year. It is no accident that some Native American ruins are located in cliffs. When visiting them, you can feel the power emanating from the ancient ceremonial kivas, as you look down over them.

Some power places are sacred because they are holy areas on Mother Earth's body. Other power centers are homes for the spirits that supervise the evolution of mineral, plant, and animal life. Shamans believe the great energy centers are inhabited by great spirits and occasionally visited by the Great Creator. Holy places must be visited always with reverence and respect. This is why the Native Americans observed certain cleansing procedures before and during their visits.

Historical power centers like Spiro National Monument in Oklahoma, Snake Mound in Ohio, Stonehenge in England, the Big Sur area in California, Chaco Canyon in New Mexico, and the mountains around Sedona, Arizona are sacred places, whether people who visit know it or not. It is dangerous to desecrate holy places.

Occasionally, an area will have bad vibrations due to certain ley lines or habitation by lower forms of spirit life. Humans with evil pasts are often stuck on earth, sometimes unable to transcend into the high spiritual planes for centuries, until karmic resolution has occurred. I have found these spirits to be most prevalent around old watering holes, underground springs, or scenes of murder or violent death, as well as areas where humans have violated nature's laws. Sometimes lower forms occupy an area where the earth's negative ley lines intersect. Unfortunately, homes sometimes are located on top of them. Never stay in any location where you experience discomfort or countless problems.

Visiting religious spots, shrines, and ancient places of worship will give you a chance to experience the vibrations of true power locations. Churches, such as the Santuario of Chamayo in New Mexico, emanate sacred energy, which you will feel as soon as you enter. These are the easiest places for beginners to learn to tune into positive energy fields because their power is contained or condensed, and therefore strong. Larger power areas have "hot spots" that generate powerful positive vibrations, but you must seek them out and they are harder to feel.

Once you know what a positive, powerful energy field feels like, you can begin to locate your own in unknown areas. To experience energy, you must take the time to clear your mind and tune in to your body as it receives the waves that are invisible but present. It may make you dizzy, like you are being gently pushed or disoriented as your body adjusts to the strong, spiritual essence. Waves of power may be experienced on your face. You will feel well, rejuvenated, and at peace. Once you know the feeling, you can explore areas close to your home and find your own place of power!

A VISION QUEST TODAY

It is possible to experience a vision quest today. It is just as valuable an experience as it was in past centuries. The vision quest is one of the oldest sacred journeys sought by humans since they gained a higher consciousness. The hunger for spiritual experiences continues in the present. In some ways, it is easier today, as less strenuous measures are necessary to communicate with our spirit guardians.

Even fifty years ago, sensory deprivation and hardship during a spiritual journey or quest were probably essential to attract your guardian angels, who live in other time and space dimensions. It used to be hard to penetrate through to these outer dimensions for spirit communication. But now, according to those interested in spiritual development, there has been a thinning of the astral veil between earth and the heavens, making it easier to make contact with our angel helpers. We have entered the Age of Aquarius, resulting in world changes and increased astral contact.

Whereas spirit communication has become easier, our earth has become more crowded and noisy, making spiritual pilgrimages more difficult. Common sense rules must be observed when pursuing solitude in an isolated area. The average person does not have the physical strength and stamina that characterized Native Americans in the past.

Imagine your physical condition if you lived outside most of your life, doing physical tasks and eating only natural food and organic game. You drank only pure water and breathed the cleanest air. Imagine never ingesting any synthetic medicines, chemicals, or additives. None of your food contained sprays or toxins. You walked miles each day on natural terrain.

This was the average way of life for Native Americans. And on top of this, they fasted, used herbs, and did colon cleansing with gourds. Many also took sweat baths in special lodges and bathed in streams and lakes to cleanse their bodies! Many Indians who greeted the white European explorers around the sixteenth century were horrified that these men did not bathe. The Indians knew, instinctively, the truth to the old cliche—cleanliness is next to godliness.

Because most of us do not have the original Native American's constitution, it is necessary to do less strenuous vision quests. There are two main methods. One is to select a "safe place" outside or in a shelter, such as a primitive cabin, in which to be alone. The second is to do a vision quest using imagery. Both methods used together, are even better. Some people like to repeat the quests routinely, at least yearly.

The Physical Quest

One necessary requirement for your physical vision quest is to be alone. The most difficult part of this quest is finding the right location. Younger, stronger people will want to stay outside in wilderness locations. Other people will want a primitive cabin in a safe, isolated area. For all wilderness quests, it is necessary to have a partner. The partner may be doing a quest, too, but this person must remain totally out of sight. It is usually best to have a meeting place where each person goes at a different time to leave a signal indicating that he or she is all right. A rock left in one spot or a piece of cloth tied to a tree limb each day is the standard signal.

People of differing ages and character types will require different types of locations, and there are many possibilities. Any place, inside or out, with a minimum of comfort and a maximum of safety and isolation, is ideal. You cannot do a vision quest in your own home unless you are an invalid. Our homes surround us with too many distractions and clues that trigger old practical thoughts and tasks. Find a location that is deserted enough for solitude but suitable for your age and physical condition.

Safe caves make effective locations for the hardy. A cave is guaranteed to make even the most concrete, or left-brained, thinker into a seer of visions. The most potent block to Americans who want to have a vision is the "left-brain syndrome." One must let go of thinking in the ordered, logical, and rational left-brained way in order to let the creative, responsive, right brain take control. Remember, a cave location demands that one take certain safeguards to avoid getting lost or disoriented. Again, a partner is necessary.

The quest is a time of reflection and of delving into one's inner soul. It may provide an opportunity for your guardian angel to send you a message or to reveal itself. This message may be in thought or dream form, or a spirit person or animal may appear to you. All are valid and real. All sensations, feelings, sounds, and images may be important messages from your spirit guides. They choose to appear to you in the form that you desire and are ready to accept you.

The most important purpose of vision quest is spirit communication. Besides the seeking out of your guardian animals or spirits, other vision quests are made to gain insight or to solve problems. You hope to be given some wisdom and knowledge from your guardian spirit.

Vision quests are highly individualistic. It is important that the person state the reason for the quest frequently so that his or her intentions are clear to the spirit helpers. Be specific as to whether you wish the identification of a guardian or solutions to problems from a teacher. It is best that only one agenda be sought at a time.

Fasting should not be attempted during the quest except for those people who have had previous fasting experience. Fasting is one of the oldest methods of increasing spirituality. It is extremely valuable in furthering your spiritual development. However, we must proceed slowly because we have pollution in our bodies that was not present in humans even one hundred years ago. The average American is so full of chemicals and medicines that even a two-day fast with water could be dangerous. This is because when one stops eating, the chemicals begin to come out of the tissues and to circulate in the bloodstream.

Drinking diluted apple juice as a method of fasting (preceding a vision quest) is recommended. For those who have never fasted and are planning to do a quest, there are certain recommendations. Do not consume meat, salt, processed foods, sugar, soft drinks, desserts, or fatty or rich foods a week before your quest. Your meals should be light and consist mainly of vegetables and whole grains. However, your diet will depend upon your location and facilities. Eat only natural foods and drink pure water and juices. Changing prescription diets, of course, must be discussed with your doctor. Water must always be available for the average American during a quest (to dilute the toxins).

For the first vision quest, it is recommended that a person stay isolated for a period of two to three days. A minimum of noise is crucial. Ideally, you should not see or hear another person for the duration of the quest. You want to exclude all the noises of civilization that you can possibly omit. No phones, newspapers, televisions, radios, or tape recorders should be near. Friends cannot drop by to talk because this will ruin your journey. No activities should be planned, such as hobbies or entertainment. No recreational equipment is recommended except a notebook and pen for jotting down personal revelations. Preparation of food, if there is any, is kept to a bare minimum. Getting less sleep than is normal during the quest helps to facilitate a theta brain wave state.

Other types of vision quest experiences include the use of a float tank, isolation in a darkened room, fire walking, ropes courses, and survival training. More and more vision quest experiences, are being offered by special groups and even by travel agencies. Some of these are excellent opportunities to begin a spiritual awakening. Always trust your own instincts in any new experiences as leaders will have specialties and usually have limited knowledge in some areas.

Some people benefit from staying alone for several days. Being without company is a thrilling opportunity and a difficult one to accomplish for many people, especially those with large families. Fantastic results can be accomplished by taking a vacation in an outdoor environmental setting. No special rules or deprivation need apply. Simply take a vacation from stress and noise. This is also recommended for people who have difficulty in being alone. Make your first quest a time to be by yourself and to eat and sleep normally.

During your quest, pay special attention to any song or melody that comes to your consciousness. It may be your power song. If it is a familiar melody, analyze the words for hidden clues as to the message that your subconscious is presenting.

Keeping a diary is recommended regardless of the type of quest chosen. Later, these notes can be used to relive your experiences. It is difficult to remember specific events when you are in a strange situation or an altered state of consciousness. The deeper one goes into right-brained thinking, the less chance there is of clear recollection.

Anyone wishing to end his or her quest before the target time can do so without any problem. You just try the next time for a little longer period. A one-day quest is a valuable beginning in obtaining higher consciousness. Start out with a shorter time frame to allow yourself time to conquer your fears. This will enable you to want to extend your stay.

Whatever your quest, know that your effort will be rewarded many times over!

Chapter Four

In the dream, she walked in billowing clouds. Little Hummingbird needed no special wings, for she was light and buoyant, her legs catapulting her wherever she wanted. The young Indian dreamed of an incredible sense of freedom, existing without a real body. The feeling overwhelmed her and drove her into ecstasy, and, as she slept, her body lifted from her earthly buffalo robe. A feeling of peace and oneness with everything overwhelmed her. She dreamed of staying here forever.

To her right, her grandfather, dressed in robes trimmed in fur and bear claws, waited for her. He reached out and helped her into the flat, slender cloud that resembled a boat. The cloud moved like a canoe sailing on the current of a swift-moving river.

She sat in the front of the cloud canoe and her grandfather sat behind her and steered. The moon was full and the clouds sailed in front of the moon as if being blown by all the wind deities at once. As they passed the moon, the winds picked her up as if to sail her through the air, using her hair as a sail. The feeling of exhilaration became so strong that she felt that her lungs would burst.

A loud crack of thunder signaled the arrival of a Thunderbeing shaped like a huge bird with an eagle's head and feet. Approaching, it swooped down toward her as she floated above the canoe. She waited for its touch, unafraid, and as the bird's wing brushed her face, she felt a tremendous jolt of energy surge through her body. It knocked her back into her cloud canoe. Now she sailed the cloud boat alone and her grandfather was gone.

In his place was a Grandmother with huge feathers in her hair and strange, large moccasins on her feet. She said, "You have received much power, my child. The ancestors from the stars have sent me to you to tell you of your destiny. You will help your people in future years whenever there is need. You will be a medicine woman of great skill and power.

"You must be careful to follow the advice of your spirit helpers and your grandfather who will guide you. Danger awaits you if you do not." With this, her moccasins split and revealed giant talons that seemed to reach out for Little Hummingbird. She tried to run but a huge wind spirit blew sand in her face and tossed her, screaming, into the air.

When she awoke, her heart was racing. She clasped the edge of her buffalo skin robe and watched the light of the full moon's gleaming through the smoke hole onto her moccasins. Her grandmother slept soundly. The significance of the dream did not escape her. The great beings spoke and she would follow their direction. She, destined to be a medicine woman! She did not question the vision but fully recognized the responsibility that it involved. She knew that she must share her dream with her grandfather when he returned.

What danger awaited her? The memory of the footprints following hers up the mountain leaped into her consciousness. Who was her enemy—and why? The vision was still fresh in her mind and the question of danger haunted her as she woke at daybreak. The darkness seemed to cast more doubts and shadows. She put on her buckskin dress and moccasins. As she left the tepee, Lonely One joined her from his resting place outside the entrance to the tepee. Little Hummingbird was thankful for his presence, for she knew that he guarded her well.

The sun's rays over the mountain removed her fears as she gave a prayer of thanks to the mighty Sun Spirit. She faced the sun, knelt down in prayer, and sang a song requesting all pain and fear to be taken away. That accomplished, she could forget all problems now and concentrate on her trip to the garden. She would tell grandfather everything when he returned.

It was her job to tend to the pumpkin patch, so she and Lonely One walked toward the garden area together. Later, her aunts, who also tended the garden, appeared to remove weeds and to see that the river flowed in to water the plants. There would be a fall festival to celebrate the harvest, and the prepared pumpkins were a large part of that event.

The uncles were not involved in the gardening. She called all of the men in her family uncle, even if they were not related by blood. She called all the women aunt and they called her daughter.

The men hunted game, fished in the river, and fought neighboring tribes when problems arose. The tribe to the west did not cultivate crops and would often raid Pumpkin Vine Village around harvest time to supplement their food supply for the winter. The men prepared in advance for their onslaught by leaving some men in the village, but others needed to hunt to prepare for the coming winter months. There never seemed to be enough men to defend the village, and some crops were always lost. Lately, the Indians started burying the root vegetables in secret hiding places, which had helped reduce the losses.

Little Hummingbird loved to watch the pumpkins grow on the vine. The vines spread out with enormous tentacles before the orange blossoms burst into full beauty. After they withered away, tiny round pumpkins, looking like green peas began to grow, becoming huge, round and orange by autumn. She looked forward to seeing the big orange pumpkins in the fall, because they reminded her of the harvest moon.

Her job today was to pick some of the blossoms at their peak for her family to eat as a delicacy. Picking off select blooms allowed the others to grow larger, thereby increasing the harvest. She also planned to pick wild greens and garlic, and brought a basket with her to gather the vegetables. She came early because it was a huge field and she wanted to get them picked before the rest of the women came to the field.

She loved her aunts dearly, but she tired of hearing them talk of sewing or cooking, just as she tired of hunting tales from the men and boys. Her aunts considered her a dreamer and feared that no man would want a wife who had no skills. So, she learned some cooking skills, but they did not sustain her interest for long. She much preferred communicating with nature and with her creatures.

As she approached the field, she spied an eagle high above her circling the field. Even at that distance, she distinguished it from a hawk because of its size. She continued walking and noticed that the eagle flew closer and closer to her. It

59

eventually flew so close that she could see its golden eyes, and she instantly recalled her dream of the previous night. She had dreamed of eagles, perhaps her power animal, and here was one circling above her. Eagles rarely came this close to the earth unless they spotted prey, at which time they swooped down. She grew curious about its presence. When hunting, they stayed up higher and then swooped down instantly before the prey had time to get away. What was the prey? She had no fear of the eagle, because her grandfather had told her that unusual sightings were often higher spirit forms in disguise.

Maybe he visited her! She did not feel that an eleven year old girl, even with a dream from the spirits, would warrant a visit without a reason. She knew that when spirit animals and birds came, it was to deliver messages and warnings. Why would she need a warning? *Of course*, she thought, *it was an omen verifying the significance of her dream and her power animal*. The eagle was reassuring her by his presence.

She obviously took after her mother in attracting animals. Her mother had always drawn deer to the camp. Her gentleness and grace brought them. Except when other game animals were scarce, deer were left alone to graze and scamper. After Wounded Deer's death, however, few deer were seen in the vicinity for several years. The hunters were forced to travel increasingly long distances to find deer meat.

The hunters were careful to observe the hunting rules and could not understand why the deer had left. Had there been a transgression in the tribe toward the deer? They always sang the deer song before a hunt so that each deer would come back to life after its death. They carefully cut away the meat from the face, leaving the bones intact and never severed the tail from the hide. To do so could offend the deer spirits, leaving the tribe without deer meat. They suspected that Wounded Deer's death played a part in their leaving, but there seemed to be more involved than that.

Grandfather always said that there were two kinds of animal and bird spirits attracted to a person. The first kind was drawn to you because it liked your vibrations, which was why Wounded Deer attracted deer and deer spirits. The second type, the power animals, complemented a person's personality. For example, an eagle signified both a special person and a need for strength and protection. She knew that Grandfather had Bear as a power animal. He needed the ferocity and aggression to complement his personality, as well as its healing abilities to use in his medicine.

Maybe she was a special person, after all. An eagle as a power animal! Grandfather always had told her she was special, but she had not known what he meant. Her aunts thought that she was different because they believed she was adversely affected by her mother's death. They tolerated her quietly, without criticism, and loved her for all of her qualities. She was truly lucky, if not special. She noticed that the eagle had begun to circle upward again, becoming a small speck in the sky. Little Hummingbird had a fleeting idea that it watched what was happening below.

She spied a female monarch laying an egg on the underside of a milkweed leaf. The milkweed provided food, and only one sticky, pale green egg was laid on each leaf. In the warm heat, each egg dried and stuck to the leaf. Each female laid several hundred eggs. After several days, a tiny larva, or caterpillar, emerged and first began eating its eggshell. Food was always in plentiful supply because each caterpillar had a whole milkweed leaf to itself.

Nature provided for the growth needed in its young, and Little Hummingbird wished that life changes in humans were as well planned. As she picked select pumpkin blossoms to take back, she was startled to see two hunters walking toward the pumpkin patch. They were Coyote Tooth and Grey Badger and they seemed to be coming directly toward her! They approached, but she pretended not to see them. Grey Badger smiled broadly and her face flushed, exposing her pretension of not knowing he was there. Coyote Tooth's eyes darted back and forth but seemed strangely happy. Coyote Tooth was a healer of bones, a medicine man. His knowledge was limited to the setting and healing of broken bones but Grandfather always said that he claimed to possess more power and skill.

Coyote Tooth spoke quickly to Grey Badger as they stopped near Little Hummingbird. "Ordinarily only women carry garden baskets but as her basket is full and your arms are empty, why not carry it for her at least to the river. I will meet you at the big rock over there."

61

Little Hummingbird blushed again and thought, *A man carrying vegetables for her, and the man being Grey Badger!* Yes, this was certainly an unusual day. First, the dream, then the eagle, and now walking with Grey Badger. Could the eagle have prophesied a coming marriage?

Grey Badger had a firm, muscled body, lean and very strong. His skin was the color of golden copper and his hair was as black as night. His eyes were dark with golden flecks that sparkled like stars in the evening. He was indeed the most handsome young man in the tribe. Her Aunt Morning Star liked him, as did all the other women and girls.

The only feature she found puzzling was his lips. They seemed too thin for his rounded face and body. Glancing over at Coyote Tooth, she saw the same thin lips and realized that he had inherited those from his father. At least she saw no other similarities, for she believed that her grandfather had good reason to dislike Coyote Tooth.

Her aunt had told her something odd about Grey Badger. He was born a twin. Twins always meant bad spirit happenings and consequently one or both were always killed at birth. His twin brother had been selected to die, being the weakest of the two. Coyote Tooth, the father, performed the deed. The baby was put in a basket and left in the river to drown. After death, the baby in the basket was buried instead of being placed on a scaffold. This allowed the bad spirits to return to the Lowerworld where they would cause no more damage.

Little Hummingbird was horrified at such an act and shuddered to think what she would do if ever faced with such a dilemma. She found many of the rituals and customs of her tribe inexplicable. She could not believe in bad spirits and horrible ghosts the way that everyone else in the tribe did. It never made sense to her that the Great Spirit would have an evil counterpart. How could a baby be evil? Because she was so young, she assumed that the elders were right and never mentioned her doubts of their ideas. Grandfather had promised to tell her his opinion when she was older.

Here she was, walking along with Grey Badger, and still she daydreamed! He said nothing until they got to a honeysuckle bush covered with blossoms and swarming with hummingbirds.

"You are Little Hummingbird. Should a hummingbird not have its nectar?" He reached over and plunked a honey-suckle blossom from the vine. Using a thin piece of twine, he leaned over and tied the blossom in her hair. His hand brushed her face and his touch seemed magical, soothing and magnetic. The touch brought a yearning for him to touch her again, and she wondered if he cast a spell over her.

She looked up into his eyes and again she froze into po-sition as if she could do nothing but return his gaze. She did not move for fear that the spell would break and he would be gone. He spoke to her tenderly, "Someday I will place many more flowers in your hair."

I want to live with this man forever, she thought. *He will be my husband. No one will know of my plan, certainly not Grey Badger. In two years, I will be thirteen and ready to marry.* Many of the girls would want him, but she would not let him know she was one of them until later.

They reached the big rock where Coyote Tooth waited. She thanked Grey Badger and took the basket to carry it into the village.

FINDING YOUR POWER ANIMAL

An important milestone in the life of many Native American children was the seeking out of their power animal. Among some tribes, this was done during a vision quest. Among others, the power animal revealed itself during a dream or ritual. The power animal appeared because someone asked for it, unlike other spirit helpers who appeared spontaneously. Unless a person was a shaman, there was a need to ask the power animal to reveal itself. Power animals often approached shamans to reveal hidden powers that they possessed and would use in the future.

The power animal was used for protection, power, and for practical purposes such as locating game or giving assistance. To be without a power animal lowered one's self esteem and status.

Michael Harner, in *The Way of the Shaman*, points out that the shaman recognized the connectedness between humans and animals. "Through his guardian spirit or power animal, the shaman connects with the power of the animal world. . . . The guardian spirit is sometimes referred to by Native Americans as the power animal. . . . It emphasizes the power-giving aspect of the guardian spirit as well as the frequency with which it is perceived as an animal."

Today the power animal is considered a type of guardian angel. Whether the angel is in animal spirit form or is a human teacher in animal guise is unknown. The Native Americans were not concerned with placing their power animals in categories. To always seek the highest aims and goals in using one's power animal assures him a noble guardian.

Power animals are those who are either close to crossing over the Rainbow Bridge or who have crossed it. The Rainbow Bridge is the place of crossing from physical life to the spirit world. It is to the animals what the astral plane is to humans. Those power animals desiring to cross over toward human evolution seek out experiences that will be of service to humans. This boosts their evolution.

Guardian angels that already have crossed the Rainbow Bridge can choose the form in which they will appear. They may appear as animal, bird, or human. The higher teachers who appear as animals are rarely found in the animal whose shape they have assumed. They appear in the form most appropriate for the person and his or her environment.

There are many levels of spiritual attainment in animals, just as

Bear Mystic *The bear was a very sacred animal to Native Americans. They made special prayers and apologies to the bear spirits before they went on a bear hunt.*

Soft Shoulders (*above*)   *When American Indian children reached puberty, they were expected to go on a vision quest during which they would receive a vision from their spirit guide. Here, a young Indian woman listens to her bird guardian.*

Night Hunter (*opposite page*)   *Native Americans believed that those people who had owl's-spirit guardians possessed great powers of divination.*

Eagle Medicine *This medicine bundle is made from an eagle skin stuffed with cedar bark and tied with buckskin strips. It is adorned with kingfisher skins, turquoise, and eagle feathers, all of which are prominently displayed to show their importance to medicine rites.*

there are in humans. They draw from their own experiences and from former evolutions, always seeking higher planes. Guardian angels seek to serve you in any way they can. However, the animal guardians are limited to the physical plane and to practical matters and the teacher guardians are interested in more esoteric questions and issues. Ideally, one needs a variety of guardian angels with as many different skills as possible.

Animal guardian angels like to care for pets and homes. They furnish totems and items representing power and protection. They like to find lost items, heal physical wounds, and help take care of pets and plants. They will guard your car and home and keep unwanted energies and problems away. Sometimes they appear to issue a "wake-up call" or increase your awareness of what is happening around you.

Just as you need different guardian angels, you also need different power animals. Your first power animal is the most important and should complement your personality. Additional power animals will represent different attributes and qualities, providing you with helpers with varied talents. You always will be in control of your power animals and they always will be helpful. If you decide to not use their services, they will drift off and seek others to serve.

DREAMING YOUR POWER ANIMAL

It is necessary to get into the habit of remembering your dreams before you ask your power animal to visit you. Otherwise, an important contact might not be remembered. To get in this habit, start a dream journal. Set it and a pen by your bed close to an easily turned on lamp. Lamps can be fitted with an attachment so that they turn on when you touch them with your hand. This is handy in the dark and requires less effort.

Set your alarm for one to two hours before you ordinarily wake up. This is the time you do your deepest and most meaningful dreaming, for you are in a delta brain-wave state. Alcohol and central nervous system depressants interfere with reaching this state, so none should be consumed at least several nights before you wish to remember a dream.

Should you be dreaming when the alarm sounds, record your

dream in your notebook before getting out of bed. Any activity will interfere with your remembering the dream. After recording it, go back to sleep, after setting your alarm if you have to get up at a certain time.

In the morning, analyze your dream content for messages. Sometimes, your first contact with spirits will provide you with an important message that you will not want to miss. In addition, you will receive important messages that portend the future. Pay careful attention to these dreams because they will give you valuable information. Write down your dreams on a regular basis. After a while it will not be necessary to set your alarm early because your unconscious will get into the habit of releasing material, and you will remember dreams upon awakening.

Before going to bed, look around the house at all the pictures, figurines, and other representations of animals you have around you, including jewelry and slogans on shirts. Browse through pictures and books of animals. Watch for programs or movies that seem to appear at about the time you are interested in contacting your power animal. Do not entertain any previously conceived notions about the identity of your first animal, because this could ruin your experience. Have a totally open mind and an intense desire to learn.

As you prepare for bed, repeat the statement to yourself of your need for a power animal guardian angel. Ask it to appear in your dream. Request that it tell you how it will help you. Ask for its appearance as you drift off to sleep. Do this for as many nights as is necessary to have your dream.

If you need extra assistance, then purchase a deck of animal cards, medicine cards, or a book with animal pictures. Do not use cards or pictures of domestic animals. They cannot be power animals. Native Americans believe that animals tamed by humans have lost their spiritual power base. Before you go to sleep, hold each card or picture up to your face, making sure that the name or picture faces away from you. Go through the assortment until you have a warm feeling when one of the pictures is next to your face. Repeat the process and see if the same picture or pictures give you a sensation of warmth or interest. Narrow down your choices until you select one card or picture.

Before going to bed, take this animal picture and talk to it. "You have a special interest in my welfare. You may not be my power animal but you can help me find it. I will look at you now with intense desire for your help (stare at picture). I can imagine touching you and talking with you. Thank you for your help. Now, I will go to sleep, knowing that I have a helper."

Remove all preconceived ideas as to which animal would be a good advisor or power animal. As in all spiritual contact, you must let go to "let it happen" or it won't. You must be prepared to receive information that you may not want to hear. Fear also will block the experience. If you are afraid, then wait before pursuing your power animal. You can do it later or never; it is your decision. Resistance is a common reaction to discovery. This is readily overcome when a person makes up his or her mind he or she is ready for the experience.

Animal Analysis

If an animal appears to you in a dream, it is significant and it may be your power animal. If it was angry or bared its teeth or fangs, it is not your guide. Also, insects cannot be power animals. If the dream was especially vivid and "felt right," then you have found your animal or bird. Remember, your first animal guide is the most significant because it tells you the most important deficiency in your personality. The type of animal that you dream complements your personality, showing you the quality you most need to cultivate. The following chart will give you some ideas as to why your particular spirit bird or animal has appeared.

Bird/Animal Type & Interpretation

Mouse   The quietness and nonintrusive qualities of the mouse will give you knowledge that is impossible to see right now because of a tendency to talk rather than obtain insight.

Wolf   Family needs are being neglected for matters not as important.

Horse   Your personal freedom is being suppressed. Letting loose and taking risks are important.

Frog/lizard   Your experiences are too mundane. Expand your awareness to include the occult and spiritual.

Skunk   You need more protection and defenses.

Badger   Someone is pushing you and you are not fighting back.

Owl   You have tremendous psychic potential that you have not developed.

Beaver   Get your lazy bones going to complete that important project.

Fox   You need to get more wily and lose your naiveté.

Raccoon   You need to get organized and also have more fun.

Ram   Seek spiritual instead of material pleasures.

Wild hare   Take time to be gentle and to smell the roses.

Eagle/hawk   You are being guided by higher spiritual forces. Important lessons and growth will happen to you.

Songbird   Beauty and aesthetics are missing in your life.

Crow   You will need help in discovering a betrayal.

Moose/elk   You need more contact with the opposite sex for a better balance of male/female energies.

Large cats   Strength and persistence are needed to accomplish goals.

Turtle/tortoise   Patience is absolutely necessary at this time. Slow down.

Dolphin/whale   Expand your awareness beyond your home and self. Community concerns need your attention.

Deer   You have a need for beauty and gentleness in your life. Let others have control for awhile.

Bear   You are a natural helper and person with power but you are not using these qualities.

Buffalo   Leadership is your hidden talent but it needs developing.

Elephant   Mental capabilities are keen but neglected. Neglect the physical for awhile in order to develop your mind.

Coyote   You need more fun in your life.

Snake   Old and ancient wisdom is yours—unused knowledge is sinful. May also indicate untapped sexuality.

Sea gull   You lock yourself into old patterns and routines. Take risks to break out of them.

Additional power animals may be acquired later. It is unlikely that they will complement your personality to the extent that your first one will. However, they will provide help and skills needed by you during those times. Power animals come and go depending upon the extent to which their help is used. Future animal helpers are acquired in the same manner as the first—you must ask for them.

Finding Your Power Animal Through Imagery

Another method of finding your animal spirit guide is to take your vision quest through imagery. Dr. Michael Harner was the first to write about vision quest imagery, which he adapted from a ritual of the Jivaro people of Peru and Ecuador. The imagery quest is surprisingly easy for most people. Drumming is used as a device to assist in achieving the necessary trance state. Research suggests that drumming puts one quickly into a theta brain-wave state, thus facilitating visions.

Dr. Harner does not like to give too many specifics or suggestions for those attempting their first journey, because he believes that it influences the findings and makes them less individualized. Option One for finding your animal, listed below, follows this philosophy. It is important to avoid disturbing a person while he or she journeys, as it could cause some soul loss. Soul loss occurs when a part of our essence or being remains in another place even though our physical body returns.

Eileen Nauman, a Cherokee Metis, prefers specific information for those journeying as it pertains to the animal selection, such as that discussed in Option Two of finding your animal.

While you are making your imagery journey you should be accompanied by a friend vigorously playing a drum or by an audiocassette of shamanic drumming. Ideally, the drum should be of sufficient quality to give a loud deep sound. Tell the friend to drum briskly for fifteen minutes, then signal the beginning of your return back with seven rapid beats followed by a pause (repeated four times), and then increase the speed of the drumming for several minutes during your return. This rapid beat signals your return from the underworld to the middle world where you live. Your completed return is accompanied by the drummer again beating seven rapid beats and pausing (four times) at the end.

All journeys are best taken in a darkened room or with a covering over your eyes to block light. Recline on the floor (using pillows if you wish) and wear comfortable clothing so there will be as few distractions as possible.

Read the following instructions for your journey and be sure to remember the main points. Use only one option each time you search for a power animal.

Getting to the Lowerworld

I want you to think of an opening that extends down into the earth, such as a cave, a natural spring, or an animal hole in a tree or the ground. The hole becomes large enough for you to enter and you do so, continuing to go down, farther and farther. You go down and down and down. You will be able to smell and feel vividly as you see yourself journeying. Eventually, you will emerge from the opening. You are now in the Lowerworld, where your guardian spirit or power animal is waiting for you. Be aware of the sights, sounds, and smells of the landscape around you. Touch something if you like. (This process will take much longer than it seems here.)

Choosing Your Animal

Option One: Keep requesting your power animal to appear until it does. It will have to appear several times to indicate its dedication to you. You cannot choose an insect, or any fish, reptile, or animal with fangs or bared teeth. After finding your power animal (no dialogue is necessary), you may bring the animal out with you or leave it in the Lowerworld. The latter is recommended for your first power animal retrieval.

Option Two: This method is recommended for those experienced in achieving imagery or trance states or those who already have done a power animal retrieval. (The dialogue is easier to handle and less likely to influence or interfere with your vision.)

Soon you will see animals around you. If you do not see any, ask your power animal to appear. Be firm in repeating your request that your animal reveal itself to you. If the animal is on your left side, walk on by. If it comes up behind you, walk away. The only animals that can come from those directions are creatures such as gophers or snakes. If the animal is in front of you or on your right side, it may be your ally. It must have either black, shiny eyes, gold, sparkling eyes, or red eyes. Red eyes are indicative of older primeval allies. Any other color will be unsatisfactory.

You should ask the animal three questions.

1. What is your name?

2. Will you obey every instruction I give you?

3. How will you help me improve myself?

If the answers to all three questions are satisfactory, turn your back and walk away. The animal must reveal itself to you several more times before you can be sure of its use to you. (When the original animal appears again, it may come from any side.) If the answers to any of the questions are unsatisfactory, thank the animal for coming, but say that you are not interested in it at this time. Be firm in order to make it leave.

If the animal appears to you several more times, you may leave the Lowerworld with it. Be sure that you close the door to the Lowerworld behind you so that no other animal will follow you out. You will come back up the path and exit from the hole or cave where you entered.

Do not be discouraged if you do not find your power animal on your first attempt. Sometimes it take several journeys before you make contact. With practice, you will find it easy to take a journey whenever you like! Be sure to write down the results of your journey.

Chapter Five

Bushyhead waited several days before meeting with the chief and the elders to tell them about the future healer. He had no intention of revealing the identity of the person, he simply wanted to reassure them that a gifted person would serve them in the future. No mention was made of his enemy, Coyote Tooth. Unprovable accusations might divide the tribe and, paradoxically, give Coyote Tooth more influence or supporters. Bushyhead felt sure that his power and his secret transfer of knowledge to Little Hummingbird would be all the protection that they needed.

Immediately upon his return to Pumpkin Vine Village, Little Hummingbird eagerly told him of her vision announcing her future as a medicine woman for the tribe. "Did you tell anyone else?" he asked quickly.

"No, grandfather, I dared not be so presumptuous as to assume that this was a prophecy until I spoke with you."

"Do not speak to anyone else of this vision," he told her. "Several older people in the tribe are coveting my position and I do not want them to know that you will be my successor until you are older and have more power. There would be jealousy if this knowledge came out, which could cause problems in the tribe."

The words *my successor* rang in her ears. Stunned, Little Hummingbird sat motionless.

"Are you all right, my child? This is a great honor for you and also for me, because I have the privilege of passing my knowledge on to you and of revealing your identity to the tribe. But we must wait until the appropriate time for the reasons that I mentioned. You are to tell no one of your destiny, not even your grandmother or Aunt Morning Star, even if they suspect the truth. Do you understand?"

She nodded and then spoke quietly. "This vision was unexpected, but very exciting, my grandfather. Did you know of my future destiny?"

"I suspected as much, but did not know for sure until I made the pilgrimage to my place of power. There, much wisdom was revealed to me. At a later time, I will share all of the experience with you. Now you must trust me and do what I say. I know you will, just as I know you will make a powerful medicine woman for the tribe," he answered.

"Tomorrow, we meet at dawn before the healing ceremony. I will explain what I want you to do during the ritual, as the first part of your training. Because you will be trained in secret, you must be subtle in your gestures during the ceremony. However, you will begin to assist in the healing process, even though others won't be aware of it. Bless you my child. The spirits walk with you."

That night, Little Hummingbird was too excited to sleep. Earlier, she had not eaten her cornmeal mush mixed with berries because her stomach fluttered and refused the sensation of hunger. She knew that she would regret it later because tomorrow she would fast in preparation for the healing ceremony. One's medicine was more powerful on an empty stomach. Sometimes, her grandfather would not eat for three or more days before an important ceremony or healing.

She would watch Bushyhead carefully during the ceremony, and he would explain more after it. A secret training certainly made it harder to learn. She did not want to bring conflict in the tribe because she was so young. It was always difficult for her when someone was mad at her. The responsibility of medicine woman was awesome enough without dissension from the elders. Her grandfather warned her that jealousy was a common accompaniment to power. The ability to watch your enemies without reacting to them would come with maturity.

Her thoughts drifted to Grey Badger. How would he feel married to a medicine woman? She was embarrassed with such a thought, for certainly nothing had happened to indicate a betrothal at this time. The idea contained so much emotion and hope that it refused to go away and she found herself contemplating the idea. Surely she would seem more desirable as a wife when he found out that she'd be a medicine woman. Or would there be the opposite reaction? She suspected that some men shunned women with power, thinking that it made them look weaker in the eyes of others.

She began to get a taste of the negative aspects that accompanied her power. Now she experienced a conflict between learning about spirituality and creating jealousy in the tribe. She hoped that she never had to choose between her spirituality and her personal life! What a tragic occurrence that would be. No, she would not think such a thing, for to dwell on trouble often brought it to you. From now on, she would entertain good thoughts about her husband wanting a medicine woman. With good thoughts of love and medicine on her mind, Little Hummingbird drifted off to sleep. The last thing she remembered was the sweet smell of piñon wood wafting through the tepee.

She crept out of the tepee just before daybreak. She could hear the mockingbird's early song encouraging the sun over the mountain. She stepped quietly over sleeping Aunt Morning Star, who had grown used to the strange comings and goings of this child of the woods. Little Hummingbird shuddered as she opened the tepee, feeling a chill, even though the weather was quite warm even for summer. Strange, she thought. It also seemed that Lonely One was gone whenever she needed him. She feared that he would wake the sleeping villagers when she journeyed to meet grandfather in secret, so she had let him stay with her uncle on the other side of Pumpkin Vine Village. It began to seem that the best way to do one thing conflicted with the best way to do another! Was this some test from the star people?

As she approached the river, where she would take a sharp turn right, she heard a twig snap behind her. She whirled quickly to look around but the darkness made it impossible to distinguish anything in the shadows. It was probably just a deer scampering for cover, she thought. She often wondered if her mother would ever appear as a deer to watch over her or if Wounded Deer ever looked down on her from where she dwelled with the Grandmothers and Grandfathers. Or had she gone to stay with the star people?

With this question on her mind, she came upon her grandfather praying alongside a mossy boulder. She had so many burning questions for him to answer. How would there ever be time to learn all of the knowledge that her grandfather wanted to teach her? Her respect for his wisdom grew daily.

74

Bushyhead welcomed her and asked her to join him in meditation. He prayed to the spirits for guidance and to the great powers for strength to heal and to help him teach his young student. Little Hummingbird felt her stomach growl and hoped that grandfather did not hear it or notice her shifting positions as her knees ached with fatigue. She prayed for patience and grace from the spirits.

The old medicine man explained, "First, I will perform rituals that enable me to see into the fourth dimension. I will blow sage over the sick body to clear the air of the impurities that block psychic vision. Then I will use my sight to see the problem area. I will also use my hands to feel the spot and to help discern the extent of and reason for the damage.

"You will notice that I will go into a trance state, which is helped by the drumming and the chanting of the singers. Blowing the sage also provides help, as does calling the spirits with my rattle. When I am performing, I want you to let go and focus on the patient yourself, as if you too were in a trance state. I will ask all family members present to come up and sprinkle herbs over his body. At that time, you will practice running your hands over his energy field to see if you can pick up any damage or problem in the body. When you return to your seat, resume the trance state and try to see beyond this sight into the special vision.

"After the ceremony, we will talk of visions and I will give you more information. We are fortunate to have a family member in need of attention at this time. Otherwise, it would arouse suspicion to have a maiden of your age attend the ceremony. As you know, only family members will be admitted. Bless you, my child. You are truly an angel in a young woman's body, sent by the star people to help the tribe after I am gone.

"Before the ceremony, continue your fasting. You are not old enough to attend the sweat lodge without some questions being asked. After your moon ceremony, you will be able to attend the sweat lodge for family members and of course, as medicine woman, you will preside over the cleansing lodge both before and after certain ceremonies.

"Before each healing ceremony, you will bathe and wash your hair. Scrape your skin with flat bones as you bathe to remove dead energy and to revitalize your body. When possible, bathe in cool water and finish under the waterfall, even in the winter. After washing, sit in the sun and ask for the mighty sun spirit to bring healing energy into your body. After more prayers, you will be ready for the ceremony.

"As you know, I asked you not to eat meat for three days before the healing event. Because birds are your natal (guardian from birth) and power animal, you will avoid the eating of all birds from now on, except for times that you need extra power and protection. During those times, you will make extra prayers to the Bird Beings and ask for their strength. Otherwise, take the bird meat others offer you and then feed it to Lonely One when no one is looking. No one must suspect your shaman status.

"You must never pluck the feathers from birds being prepared for cooking. You must never be in the presence of the women who cook or prepare bird meat. To do so would be dangerous to your power, for such practices offend your guardian spirits. Any bird meat you eat will be prepared by another and served to you only at daybreak on the morning that you desire the extra power. On those days you continue to fast because, for you, bird meat is spiritual energy, not food.

"It is important to eat a good diet for optimum vitality and healing energy. Vegetables and grains are important, as are wild greens and berries. Meat, other than bird meat, is important during the winter and times of extra stress and after fasting.

"You must also begin using gourds as utensils to clean your bowels. This will be important from now on because you must lighten your physical density. This will also lower your spiritual density, making spirit communication and travel much easier. Go now and begin your preparations."

Little Hummingbird left her grandfather to his praying. Walking toward the river, she spied a striped caterpillar crawling on a leaf. It had black, yellow, and white stripes. The caterpillar had eaten half a milkweed leaf and sat sunning itself on the remainder of its sticky carpet. While she watched, it puffed up its head, splitting its old skin as its head burst out. It turned its black, horned head and began eating its old skin. She was astonished—it seemed so easy for a caterpillar to shed its old image and assume a new one.

Changing her old skin for her new powerful image would

be difficult but exciting. Still feeling the joy in her heart, she looked forward to bathing in the river. Before she entered the river she would fill gourds with water and use them to cleanse her bowels. Being a medicine woman was certainly not all power and beauty. The physical body needed attention to bring it to higher levels, and she knew that the procedure brought about higher spiritual communication.

After completing this task, she dove into the river and swam toward a waterfall that her grandfather had told her to visit. She washed and scraped her skin and then stood under the waterfall to complete her cleansing just as her grandfather had instructed. The marvelous Water Babies removed all earthy vibrations and replaced them with glowing sensations.

She enjoyed her shower, lifting up her arms in exhilaration. Afterwards, Little Hummingbird dressed in her light buckskin dress and sat on a rock to sun herself and to dry her hair. As she combed her hair with a tortoise shell, voices interrupted her solace. Grey Badger and his friend, Mad Fox, discovered her sitting on the boulder. Spiritual as she felt, her eyes flashed when she saw him, and she was conscious of her body position, her long black hair fanning out around her like a posturing peacock.

He spoke. "My father, Coyote Tooth, said you were going to be in a healing ceremony today for your uncle. I wish him luck in receiving help and cure. I hope to talk with you about the healing ceremony, because I fear my grandfather will soon need one. I wish to learn all that you observe your grandfather doing. Could we meet down here in four days after the ceremony is over? I will return from the hunt about the same time." He seemed distant, as if his message was rehearsed. She believed he was embarrassed to talk with her in front of Mad Fox, who tried to appear uninterested in the conversation.

It was her turn to appear as if this were a routine conversation. She said she would be at the river in four days, washing family garments from the healing if he wished to find her. She would discuss her uncle's condition and the healing results.

He spoke further. "We are going into dangerous territory to hunt buffalo. Only the best braves will go. Mad Fox and I were selected, and this will be our first mission to demonstrate bravery. If I get a chance, I will kill my first buffalo."

Little Hummingbird was unsure of his intentions. Did he need to prove himself to her or was he testing to see if she feared for his safety? Or both? She smiled and said she would like to hear all about his adventure when she shared the news of her uncle. This seemed to satisfy him, for when his friend tugged at his quiver stuffed with arrows and signalled a desire to leave, Grey Badger waved and said, "Goodbye, until four mornings from now."

As always, she felt a wave of depression when he left. Realizing her condition, she knew she must again stand under the waterfall to remove all earthy wishes and desires. How could she be a medicine woman if she remained interested in only matters of the heart and body?

Under the waterfall, she imagined that all her earthly problems, shortcomings, faults, weaknesses and bad vibrations were washed away through the power of the Water Babies. Returned to the highest state of spirituality she could obtain at the time, she again sunned herself and prayed to the Sun Father for energy and help in healing her uncle. Even while praying, she realized the difficulty of maintaining higher order thoughts without thinking about Grey Badger. He continued to penetrate her consciousness. She had indeed discovered her biggest obstacle to achieving her own spiritual power!

CLEANSING THE SURROUNDINGS

Before beginning to diagnose or heal illness, always cleanse the room and the people in it with the smoke of sage or cedar. The dried leaves may be bound together in a smudge stick or crushed into a pile that is dense enough to smolder. Both sage and cedar grow wild in most areas and are easily obtained. Never overpick your source and never pick during times of drought. Always ask permission from Mother Earth to pick the leaves and always leave the root intact.

The best way to obtain sage or cedar is to purchase it from businesses marketing smudge sticks that take environmental concerns into account. When possible, check their sources and find out how they replenish their supplies or if they grow them. You also can buy sage from nurseries or grow your own in an herb garden. Cedar is more plentiful in the wild and is easily grown in your yard. Be careful to ask permission and not damage the trees.

Once you obtain your sage or cedar, light it and then blow out the flame so that it smolders and throws off smoke. Put it in a container that is bigger than the smudge so that there is no danger of fire. Light it in a place where any loose spark won't ignite the surroundings. Only use very small amounts so that the sparks and smoke are contained. Using a feather fan or other spreading device, make sure that the smoke permeates whatever you are cleansing. It is best to start with the room. Then, fan the smudge onto both the front and back of the person who is to be worked on. Smoke yourself by setting the smoldering sage down and turning your front and back toward it to cleanse yourself. You can use a fan to help cover yourself.

Draperies or upholstery will absorb the resins from the smoke, so do not overdo your cleansing. It is not necessary to fill the room with smoke or to make anyone cough or be uncomfortable. A little smoke is powerful and goes a long way toward cleansing both room and people of undesirable vibrations.

THE FEELING DIAGNOSIS

The feeling analysis for trouble spots in the body is done with the hands. You will not touch the person, only his or her aura, which-will be out several inches to a foot or more from the body. By moving your hand gently toward the person, thereby compressing the space between your hand and the person's body, you will be able to feel different sensations. Unless you can see auras, you will be analyzing solely from touch. Remove all jewelry and only wear clothing made of natural fibers when doing your analysis. Ask your client to put any jewelry in a purse or billfold.

You will check for hot spots, cold spots, dead spots, power spots, vibrating spots, and sensations in your own hands, such as tingling or numbness. The different sensory feedback and its meaning will be subjective. As you begin to use your hand, you will form your own data for interpretation. It will be necessary to practice before you analyze with skill. However, many people can locate troublesome areas in the body the first time they try.

Cold spots mean a blocked or congested area. The colder the area, the more blockage there is. It is interesting that the name for the common cold also describes the sensation that it produces in the hands. Feel the aura over the face of a person who has a cold and you will feel the chill. Cold spots may indicate chronic problems where circulation is impaired or blockages are present. These closed areas can be improved with healing energy. As you might suspect, the physical and emotional auras can be affected with problems in any area.

Hot areas are more serious and indicate longterm tissue damage or auric shutdown. They may indicate diseased or "burned out" areas. These are usually characteriological , meaning characteristic of a person with a particular personality and physical constitution. A hot aura around the head may indicate a person who focuses on the negative or has a chemical imbalance or pituitary weakness. A hot spot in the pelvic area may mean disease or an obsession with sex.

Flat or dead spots represent a lack of vitality or emotion, usually due to repression. Physically, they may signify organ removal or surgery. Flat spots in the pelvic area may mean the person has had sexual organs removed or has no sex life.

Diffuse scattered vibrations often indicate that a person has conflicting intentions or is confused. These areas may indicate an inherent weakness in the body or a tendency to be nonfocused or indecisive. There may also be static electricity, which interferes with receiving positive electrons and brings discord.

If one hand tingles or feels numb, check out the same spot with the other hand. This is usually indicative of static electricity or of problems in the body. If so, more analysis is needed to determine the reason.

Occasionally, you will encounter a person whose aura is so powerful that you feel the pressure of it pushing against your hands as you attempt to compress inward. This may mean a healer or person of tremendous spiritual energy, or it may mean a person who is extremely emotional and is propelling all his or her vitality outward.

In order to make a differential diagnosis, you need the person's permission and cooperation. As will be discussed later, questions and inquiries are helpful. Intrusive questions are unnecessary, because the person will usually volunteer the information that you need. Never show any emotion if something feels bad or serious. Because all work is experimental and your ethics do not permit scaring someone, quietly comment and ask for further information. No matter how skilled you become, it is not your place to offer differential diagnosis. Your analysis also could be incorrect. Assessment is done to locate areas that are in need of healing and to offer general feedback to the person so if he desires, he can continue improving himself.

Before you begin your analysis, take a deep breath through your nose and breathe out through your mouth. Repeat this breathing several times and, while you are doing this, picture vines rooted deeply in the earth entwining your ankles to anchor and center you. Picture the sun coming from the other direction (above you) and encapsulating you in a golden cocoon of healing energy. Imagine this vital solar energy coming down into you through the top of your head.

The above exercise will help to keep your resources from being depleted and will give you more available healing energy. It will also ground you. Vibrations received from above insure healing energies from high sources so that you don't have to use your own and grounding insures that all undesirable energies will not stay in your body. This is particularly important for "givers," who frequently expend too much of their own energy and end up depleted. Working on the auras of others without these steps can be dangerous.

If, after following these steps, you find yourself exhausted or weak, you need to delay your healing career until you have strengthened your own aura and removed negative influences from around you. If you continue working with other people's auras, you could deplete your energy supply to such dangerous levels that you would not have the resources to throw off negative material and literally could catch another person's problem.

After doing your breathing and grounding exercises, you are ready to begin your feeling diagnosis. Explain to the person that you want him or her to practice breathing in and out calmly while you feel the vibrations around his or her body. Tell the person that he or she can either leave his or her eyes open or close them and that you will begin at the back and move to the front.

As you move your hands, you will be no closer than several inches from the person's body. You may want to come out eight or nine inches or more at certain times. Begin by doing an overall assessment with both palms simultaneously, making sure that your fingertips are pointing up and you are facing the back of the person. Move your hands together in unison and sweep across the back area beginning at the head and coming down. When you get lower, you will want to reverse your palms so that the fingertips are down. Do this slowly enough to measure any sensations. Then switch to the front and work your way down. I usually start by having the person sit down and then ask the person to stand when doing the back side. If the person is tall, ask him or her to sit while you do the head and shoulder area from behind.

This preliminary assessment will give you a general idea as to a person's energies. Let your mind be as clear as possible and note any thoughts that enter your mind at the same time you are feeling with your hands. Remember, do not touch the body—you should be out at least several inches from it.

The next movement focuses on specific sensations and is done with one hand on one side of the body and the other hand on the other side of the body. You will be facing the side of the person. You will examine the whole body as well as the chakras. This technique is valuable because you can check out a sensation felt with one hand by switching to the other. Sometimes I ask the person to turn slightly if I am checking out drafts in the room. If you experience the same sensation with the other hand, then you have verified your data.

Begin this analysis by coming down from the top several feet above the person's head and working closer to the crown. Check the crown chakra without pushing too hard on that area. Proceed slowly, stopping when you feel compression against your hands. If you press down too hard and too close it could be uncomfortable for the person. If you feel resistant pressure at eight or nine inches, stop there.

After doing the crown chakra, come down, still keeping one hand on each side, and measure the third-eye chakra. One hand is level and perpendicular in front between the eyes and the other hand is behind the head at the same horizontal level. While in this area, check the head, switching sides with your hands before moving on. Mentally note what you find. Do not comment on any findings until after you have completed your analysis.

After moving down from the head, survey the shoulders and the top of the chest. The throat chakra is checked separately. Again, avoid pushing too forcefully against it. If you feel significant sensations, rotate both hands (attempt to duplicate sensation with the other hand) and ask the person to move slightly. This helps guard against any sensations that might be coming from your own hand or from any draft in the room.

The heart chakra is assessed next with the lower half of the chest. One hand will be in front of the heart and the other will feel the back at the same level. At this point, ask your client to stand for the examination of the lower half of the body.

The solar plexus chakra is right above the navel. Check this area along with the abdomen. The root chakra is at the base of the spine. Again, test both front and back locations at the same time. Sensations are double-checked by switching hands. After completing the torso, finish by going down both legs to the feet.

Now you have completed your examination. Depending on the client, you may ask a few questions as you proceed. Notes are helpful if numerous problem areas are located. Otherwise, delay all comments and questions until completion of the diagnosis.

After surveying the whole body, go back and discuss any difficulties that your client has experienced in relation to the particular areas that you have flagged. Say as little as possible about your finding and use words like "cold spot" or "hot spot." It will not help anything if you tell your fears or dramatic findings.

A person cannot tell you the condition of his or her chakras and you may or may not want to share what you have discovered. If, however, you are going to do any healing on that chakra, then it is imperative that you ask the person's permission and share your findings so that he or she can give consent to your healing work. This will keep you out of the realm or working in secret and will include the client in the healing and awareness process, making your healing more effective.

You will discover a relationship between the physical (etheric) and emotional (astral) auras. Difficulty in one area always results in repercussions or accompanying problems in the other.

A closed or blocked third-eye chakra may mean panic states or someone with tunnel vision. Such a person may have had chemical imbalances or suffer from depression or manifest denial.

A cold throat chakra tells you that the person does not say what he or she thinks. A cold heart chakra may reveal a person who has closed off emotions for protection. A hot area may mean disease or malfunction in the organ or glands. Heart and heart chakra problems are often related to inabilities to give and receive love, problems usually developed during childhood.

Solar plexus sensations indicate control issues or holding in of negative emotions. This includes fear and anger. Resultant effects are reflected in the liver, kidneys, small intestines, and stomach.

The lower chakra demonstrates problems in the sex organs, urinary tract, and appendix. This area is important to a person's stability and security.

Other locations on the body such as the thigh or knee, will reflect difficulties in that area.

The healer never pretends to be a physician or other kind of healer. He or she is simply doing a spiritual analysis that may or may not yield information to be of assistance to someone. Never make claims or say that you will treat any disease. It is better if no specific disease is mentioned by you. Never agree to treat a certain problem or suggest that the person stop seeing his physician.

After all, your treatment is an energy procedure and has nothing to do with a particular problem or with treating certain disorders. Any healing or assistance you do is only through light and energy channelled down from high sources. Therefore, any healing done is not enacted by you personally.

After analysis, begin healing. It is not necessary to know a reason for the problem or even have an idea why areas demonstrate certain sensations. You merely identify these areas so you will know where to concentrate your healing energies. Any insight about the difficulty is for the client to use for increased awareness.

Before you begin again, repeat your exercise of deep breathing—in through your nose and out through your mouth. Imagine vines rooted deeply in the earth entwining your ankles to anchor and center you. Picture the sun coming from above your head and encapsulating you in a golden cocoon of healing energy. Feel this vital solar energy coming down into you through the top of your head and going out your feet into the ground. By having the light come down into and through your body, you protect your vitality and keep yourself from absorbing unwanted energies from your clients.

Envision this healing light coming through your hands. Place your hands several inches from the person's body in the areas that most need healing. Then go over the spot repeatedly with a downward stroking motion, keeping your hands out from the body several inches. Let the light from your hands soothe and heal this area. Feel the energy penetrating the person's body, bringing energy and health. If desired, hold your hand in a fixed position for a while before resuming your "petting" or downward stroking.

Move to the next area that must be energized. Repeat the healing process. After energizing the area, move to any others that you have found. After working on specific locations, finish your healing process by lightly stroking the whole body again in a downward motion. Remember, you are not touching the body, only the aura. This seals and closes the auras and gives the person a feeling of wellbeing.

After healing, always flick off your hands the energy that you have received and wash them with cool running water. Energy treatments may have to be repeated for best results, but wait several days or a week between treatments.

Chapter Six

Little Hummingbird sat in her isolation hut. Upon commencement of her moon, or puberty, she moved into a special tepee reserved for a girl's initiation into womanhood. This ceremony would last four days, during which time she could not have any meat or salt, nor could she communicate with others. She remained inside, seeing no one except an appointed corn mother. This corn mother revealed secret curing techniques to her. During her seclusion, Little Hummingbird ground corn, which insured her fertility and demonstrated respect for the Corn people.

When a young Indian woman was on her moon, she did not eat in the presence of others for fear of contaminating their food or damaging crops. Because Little Hummingbird was on her first moon, she was considered even more dangerous. Once, lightning had struck several members of a family when one girl did not tell of her moon. After Little Hummingbird's initiation ceremony, she would share a special grass house with other women on their moon. Now her corn mother left her food, and no one else dared enter the tepee.

A woman on her menses never slept next to her husband. If she did he could be wounded or killed in his next battle. She also avoided touching his shield or any other war implement. Menstruating women were considered to have special power that could affect others. They could never touch a medicine bundle or enter a lodge where there was a medicine bag during this time.

Snowy Hare, the cousin of Little Hummingbird, had been the last girl to sit in the secluded tepee, which was located at the southernmost end of the village. She had been sullen and resentful of her isolation. Their aunt, Morning Star, her appointed corn mother, returned from the tepee with tales of tears and loneliness during Snowy Hare's stay. Frightened by the possible implication of her charge's behavior, Morning Star had said extra prayers to the Corn spirits in order to placate them. Snowy Hare never cried audibly. Even she knew the consequences of such action. To wail openly during a moon ceremony could spell doom for the next corn harvest.

The disposition shown by a maiden during her moon stayed with her for the rest of her life. Indeed, several young warriors had expressed reluctance to marry Snowy Hare, assuming she would be sullen and difficult to be around. In addition, they feared that she would avoid work. Industrious women were considered more desirable. For this reason, Little Hummingbird, who was a dreamer, feared that she would never attract young men because of her apparent lack of industry.

After Snowy Hare's isolation period had ended, she accepted her new status as a woman of the tribe and enjoyed the privilege of attending village ceremonies for adults. Aunt Morning Star still talked of possible problems during childbirth for Snowy Hare because of her demonstrated resentment during her moon ceremony. A possible stillbirth might result. Stillborn babies were always buried beneath the mother's tepee, a practice that kept the ghost of the dead baby around.

Little Hummingbird loved the isolation. She welcomed the opportunity to communicate with her spirits and to be alone with her own thoughts. Because a taboo also existed against male animal visitors, Lonely One lingered around the tepee but got no opportunity to enter.

Her grandfather explained to Little Hummingbird the reasons behind the taboos surrounding menses. He told her that she was feared not because the blood from her body was bad, but because the blood was so powerful. This knowledge was kept from other tribal members so that no one would use such power for their personal gain.

When the secret ceremonies of grinding corn ended, she would be given a sacred grain of corn to swallow. This would ensure her fertility. Afterward, she would be bathed in the river by other women. Her hair would be washed with soapplant fibers and rinsed with water collected during the last full moon. Her corn mother would fix her hair in the style worn during special ceremonies. It would be gathered on both sides and puffed in whorls. The next and last time she would wear this style would be on her wedding day.

The seed of life contained within her newly ripe body brought thoughts and yearnings for Grey Badger. The blood flowing between her legs brought physical sensations that she had not experienced before. The spirits known as the Grandmothers prepared her for womanhood.

Grey Badger became a man several years ago. Boys of fourteen underwent four days of initiation, including a whipping ritual during the Winter Solstice ceremony. This was the only time that the boys in the tribe were whipped, and not one would consider showing any display of fear because of the shame that it would bring to their manhood. Little Hummingbird definitely preferred isolation and womanhood.

She thought back to the day she had met Grey Badger at the river as they had planned. She had awakened early that morning, excited at the prospect of talking with him after he returned from his hunting trip. She had gathered all the garments worn by her uncle and her family during the healing ceremony. It was necessary to wash them in the river to removed any remains of the sickness that her grandfather had removed from her uncle's body. Bad vibrations clung to clothing and to people. All those present used the sweat lodge after the ceremony to cleanse themselves. It was her job to wash the clothing. She had loved the smell of the sweetgrass and sage on the garments.

Little Hummingbird made sure that she was present at the river before Grey Badger and the hunting party returned from the buffalo hunt. She brought her pet, Lonely One, for company as she planned to spend the whole day waiting, if necessary. She chose a place in the river where the view was blocked off from the village side, but where she could see the returning hunters as they passed down the mountain and they could see her. She washed the clothes between two boulders for further privacy. She didn't want any of the villagers to be aware of her contact with Grey Badger. Rumors often started talk of wedding ceremonies!

She was in no hurry to begin rubbing tallow made from buffalo fat on the clothes, so she sat on a boulder and looked up toward the mountain. She wondered why her mind seemed to continue to come back to thoughts of him. Yes, Grey Badger was handsome and would make any woman proud to be his wife. But thoughts of him also brought uncomfortable sensations that were difficult to describe. She knew nothing of trusting her instinct or of the gradual development of the intuitive skills that were present in all medicine people. She feared and yearned for Grey Badger at the same time. She decided that her feelings were simply ones of excitement caused by her imminent meeting with him.

Still daydreaming on the boulder several hours later, she spotted the hunters returning, but saw that they had no meat. She jumped off the rock and quickly began washing the clothes in the river. Looking up, she saw the hunters split up and head toward their individual tepees. As Grey Badger approached, Lonely One growled. The wolf presented himself as a formidable obstacle.

"It's a friend, Lonely One. Let him pass," she said as she patted her animal on the head.

Grey Badger smiled, revealing perfect white teeth as he spoke. "Hello. How did the healing ceremony go?"

She dropped her clothes on a rock by the side of the river and waded out of the water.

"Oh, uncle is well. Thanks to grandfather." Little Hummingbird sat on a rock and dried her feet in the sun. She discussed the ceremony.

"Grandfather used sweetgrass and sage to clear the air and then began to see into uncle's body with his special vision." She caught herself saying too much about the sacred procedure and stopped talking.

"You know a great deal about healing," Grey Badger said. "I may need to know all you find out, as Coyote Tooth says that someday I will be a powerful healer."

Little Hummingbird felt a twinge of fear. She thought, *He believes that he will be the healer.* She looked up at him. *What if he finds out that I am the appointed medicine woman for the tribe?* Her heart beat rapidly.

She changed the subject. "How did the hunt go?"

"The buffalo knew of our plans and avoided us," he said, with downcast eyes. "Next time, we will perform more powerful buffalo medicine before the hunt, and I plan to kill my own buffalo."

89

Feeling his disappointment, she again changed the subject. "Lonely One has been chasing that fish in the river up and down the bank all morning." She laughed. "He thinks he is a bear or an eagle."

Spotting the large fish, Grey Badger pulled an arrow from his quiver and, with one powerful twang of his bow, neatly speared the fish through its side. Lonely One instantly swam to retrieve it, as he had been trained to do. Taking the fish from the wolf's mouth, Grey Badger handed it to Little Hummingbird.

"You can take this fish to your family," he told her. "It will make a generous meal."

"You are a good hunter, Grey Badger. Thank you for this large fish. I will prepare it tonight."

As she spoke, her hand lightly rested on his shoulder in a gesture of natural affection. Realizing her action, she started to jerk her hand away but before she had a chance, he placed his hands on both sides of her waist.

"I would like to catch you," he whispered. Little Hummingbird found that all the breath had left her body and she could do nothing but stand motionless, caught in the magic of the moment.

"Grey Badger!" Coyote Tooth spun into view. "What did you catch?"

"A fish."

Coyote Tooth looked at fish and then at Little Hummingbird. "A big fish or a little one?" He grinned slyly.

"Oh. A large one. I see. Good. This is cause for celebration." Coyote Tooth turned. "Come. Let's go and talk. Goodbye, Little Hummingbird."

As she sat in her tepee later, Little Hummingbird thought back on the feelings of that day. They had created the unfulfilled yearning in the pit of her stomach that she was now feeling. It was as if love, unsatisfied, churned in her body.

She blushed as she remembered her foolishness when she had started to talk of the secret rituals performed by her grandfather at her uncle's healing. What if speaking of the magic ruined future healings? She panicked at this thought, and her love yearnings were replaced by waves of fear. If her grandfather realized her betrayal of his trust, he never would give her special information again. What a young and foolish girl she was! On the other hand, she had revealed no information that another person could use. In the future, she never would repeat any aspect of the medicine she learned—not even to her husband.

Uncle's healing session returned to her mind. He had lost one of his wives last year, and since that time he suffered from severe back pain that caused him to be bedridden at times. It was rumored that he had not treated that wife kindly. His other wife was his dead wife's sister who had lost her husband in a battle several years before. The sisters were from the Bear Clan. Little Hummingbird and her uncle belonged to the Turtle Clan. Grey Badger was from the Owl Clan. It was forbidden to marry within one's own clan.

When Little Hummingbird entered the room during the healing, her uncle lay stretched out face down on a rug. He had not eaten for four days. Her two aunts were there, and they chanted while two men beat the drums. Her grandfather, Bushyhead, sat on his knees by the patient. His eyes were closed. Stretched out in front of him, lay his medicine bag, herbs, meat and stones.

Bushyhead also had not eaten for four days. The other relatives had fasted for one day, and sat in the sweatlodge before the ceremony. Bushyhead blew the smoke of the sacred sage and sweetgrass over the patient and used sacred feathers to waft the smoke where he wanted it. He placed some meat at the feet of the sick man and sprinkled powdered herbs around him.

Bushyhead held his hands over the man's back. Again and again, he shook sacred rattles over the place of the pain. He also chanted as he worked on her uncle's back. Bushyhead appeared to be in a daze, but continued to work over his patient. He bent over toward the man's back, then he flung his hands up and over the body before him as if to fling unwanted material out the smoke hole of the tepee. Little Hummingbird began to feel lightheaded. She was shocked to discover she could see the outline of Bushyhead's power animal, Bear, standing over the medicine man.

When her grandfather bent over to work on her uncle, the protruding shadow of Bear's face stuck out over Bushyhead's own profile.

Little Hummingbird, amazed at the sight of Bear, wondered when she would see her own power animal, Eagle.

So, the medicine to heal did come from a power animal, she thought. Because no one in the village ever mentioned seeing Bear with her grandfather, she guessed that it was not visible to others. Amazed at her perception, she now knew that she would never need to doubt her own helper as long as she did nothing to offend Eagle.

Later, she asked her grandfather this question. He stated that only those with special sight could see into the fourth dimension. She had special vision and had been selected to be the future medicine person for the tribe. Usually, a person had to be "awakened" before the sight occurred, but she may have been given the ability because of her mother's death at her birth.

Little Hummingbird asked her grandfather what had been wrong with her uncle. He said that her uncle had treated his dead wife badly and suffered guilt for his actions because he truly loved her. His guilt and his love for her caused him to hang onto her memory, thus her ghost did not want to leave. Her ghost hung onto his back, causing back pain. Her grandfather had released the ghost. She remembered seeing a shadow over her uncle's back. Bushyhead told her uncle that he must fast for two more days in the woods to ask forgiveness of the spirits for mistreatment of his wife. He was never to mention her name again, as this could cause her ghost to return. For additional forgiveness, he must be especially kind to his other wife and always be patient with her. This would help him stay released from the ghost.

As she thought about the healing, Little Hummingbird realized she had told Grey Badger little of the actual magic that had occurred. Feeling relieved, she looked upward toward the top of the smoke hole of the tepee. For the several days since her isolation, she had watched a caterpillar attach itself to the underside of one of the poles that served as part of the tepee frame. First it had spun a silky pad and attached its back feet to it so that it hung suspended upside down. Then, it began to split its larva skin for the last time. The new skin, which now formed a pupa or chrysalis, was soft and damp, and it dried a shiny green with gold dots. For now, the larva hung safely cocooned.

Little Hummingbird wondered if it was significant that a larva spun itself a cocoon during the time that she sat sequestered in her special tepee. As she contemplated that thought, she scratched her head with the special stick given to her. To touch her hair while menstruating would result in its loss. She wanted to emerge from her seclusion with beautiful hair.

When her ceremony finally ended, it was celebrated with a community festival. Her relatives brought baskets of clothes, grains, skins, and food to give to others. In turn, unrelated villagers brought gifts, which they exchanged for those in the baskets. After the gifts were exchanged, four days of celebration began, during which the women performed the feather dance and the men sang to the rhythm of the rattle.

During the celebration, one of many feasts was held where they served succotash, ash bread, buffalo meat, ground corn, and honeycakes.

Little Hummingbird led one of the dances, which was performed in a line that was composed of alternating unmarried young men and women. She kept hoping that Grey Badger would be the one behind her, but some other young warrior always got there first.

After eight days of ceremony, which included her time in isolation, Little Hummingbird was now tired, slimmer, and officially a woman.

THE MOON

The moon symbolizes feminine energy in many cultures around the world. To many Native Americans, the moon is the female Great Spirit, and the moon's influences represent female concerns and attributes. The menses are in many languages, including some European, called "moon," and many Native American women still refer to their menstrual time as "being on their moon."

On Earth, the moon controls the tides. If the moon can lift trillions of tons of water from the mighty ocean, do you suppose that it could have an effect on the pounds of water that make up a large percentage of your body? *The Farmer's Almanac* publishes detailed accounts of the moon's cycles because of their effects on the growth of crops and many people plan activities to coincide with phases of the moon.

The feminine aspect of humans is the intuitive, emotional, creative, receiving, empathic, and loving nature. Native American philosophy, like other great religions of the world, stressed the importance of the duality of human nature and the growth toward balance as a way of raising one's spiritual nature. There is negative-positive, man-woman, day-night, good-bad, and love-hate. It is desirable to achieve both emotional (feminine) and mental (masculine) qualities. One needs both right brain and left brain functioning. The special dominance of each need waxes and wanes to coincide with cyclic events in life.

In mythology, the waxing moon represents new life, beginnings, youth, innocence, creation, growth experimentation, and the prepubescent female. The full moon represents sex, fertility, power, fruition, harvest, maturity, completion, and woman. The waning moon signifies endings, death, disintegration, wisdom, evolution, transformation, destruction or reorder, and the old woman.

In astrology, the moon represents the feminine and feeling. Although most people are aware of their sun sign, few realize that they also have a moon sign (the zodiacal sign their moon was in at birth). This sign tells you how you handle your emotions and, in esoteric astrology, gives you information about past lives. The knowledge of your moon sign, and your sun sign, and your ascendant (star sign) allows your birth chart to be completed in great depth.

You can then follow your moon sign on a calendar. Remember,

it is when the full moon is in your particular sign that emotion is at a peak for you. Many bookstores sell astrological calendars for just such a purpose.

No Native American tribe identified the moon (Mother Moon) as masculine although several viewed the sun (Father Sun to most) as feminine. The impact of the aspects of our feminine nature, such as our right brains, is important for men as well as women. Just as full moon ceremonies have healing qualities for the female organs, they are equally soothing and balancing to male bodies as well. They are especially beneficial for those persons who wish to increase their sensitivity and creativity.

Full Moon Ceremony

This ceremony can be performed only by women or by a mixed group of women and men. If women alone are present, a circle is formed. If men are also present, they form a ring around the women. (It is not necessary for the men to be close together, so only a few can occupy the outside circle.) Native American men did not attend activities inside the women's isolation hut, but did take part in the community ceremonies.

The moon ceremony can also be performed by one person if desired. There is no set number for optimum effects although at least three women may be helpful to attract moon energy to the circle. The more positive people who are present, the more successful the ceremony. Negative or irreverent people will likely hinder results. It is important that the ritual not begin until all are seated in the circle. No one should leave during the ceremony or break the circle.

Ideally, the ritual should be performed as close to the height of the full moon as possible. Again, astrological calendars will provide this information. If the time is not practical, it can be done one day before or two days after the moon is at its fullest. During summer, it is best to perform the ceremony out-of-doors, because this will give it a special feeling. However, the moon has no trouble sending her special powers into your home or building.

One woman should be designated to read the following suggested script. You can make additions in order to further personalize the directions. *Each sentence is to be read slowly. Pause between sentences.* Choose a person with a low, melodious voice, if possible. Celestial music, tinkling chimes, or soothing Native American chanting will also enhance the results.

This ceremony was given to Sunne Nelson (a psychic with sight into the fourth dimension) by her Indian spirit guide, Shaw Tah Wah Nee. A Cherokee friend told her that Shaw Tah Wah Nee would appear to her in physical form. He did appear to her several weeks later, standing behind her earthly father. The spirit revealed to her that she had been his daughter in a previous life and had been named Eagle Woman. Now, Shaw Tah Wah Nee stays outside the circle when the Indian Woman Spirits join Sunne in her circle.

The ceremony should be performed sitting comfortably, with legs crossed or straight. Relax as much as possible. The script is then read slowly, as follows:

Imagine the moon above your head shining down into your head where your hair naturally parts. Visualize the moon about six inches above your head. Feel how bright and heavy it is.

See an elixir drip from the moon. Feel it slide slowly into the crown of your head. (*pause*)

Feel the elixir trickling down into your throat, down into your chest cavity, and into your stomach. Now feel it dripping down into your pelvic area. Breathe it, feel it, know it is there. See the elixir moving down your thighs and toward your kneecaps, down to your lower legs, and toward your feet. As it begins to drip out of your body into the circle, you will feel as though you are sitting in this elixir. (Stop.) See it filling up the circle. We are all sitting in this elixir and everyone's body is glowing with this beautiful light. (*pause*)

Beloved father, mother, god, bring the light shining forth to each and every person (woman/man) in the circle. Thy cup runneth over and I have spoken in your name.

Now, I want you to begin to breathe slowly and deep. Take very even breaths. Raise your arms up toward the moon with palms facing outward. Reach for the moon. Call forth its energy to come into your body.

Give thanks in each and every way for the light that the moon gives us. Now bring your hands down on your knees and rest them there. Now I want you to visualize the moon beaming down this elixir in energy form, in little sparkles, and bring it into the center of your palms. As you breathe in, breathe in the energy from the moon, and when you breathe out, feel the energy still coming into the palms of your hands. (*long pause*)

Take your left hand and place it on top of your head, palm down; place your right hand, palm toward you, on your third eye, which is between your eyes in the center of your forehead. Breathe in, and as you breathe out, allow the energy from your hands to be released from your hands into your head area.

You are now going to bathe your chakras with the white light of the moon. Breathe in and breathe out, cleaning and clearing away all the debris, all the mental anguish and distress, filling your beautiful head with beautiful light. (*pause*)

Take your left hand from the top of your head and place it on your throat, leave the right hand on your forehead, bathe your throat with this energy, breathe in deep and breathe out, let the air come slowly out of your mouth. (*pause*)

Now, I want you to take your right hand and gently place it on your heart. Leave your left hand on your throat. Blow all negativity out of your body, breathe in light, breathe out with a slight noise through your mouth. Let go. Let go. Let go. Breathe out again. Now, move your left hand from your throat, down over the stomach, leaving the right hand on the heart. Breathe in elixir, breath out stress. (*pause*)

Relax your shoulders, leaving the hands on the body, relax those stomach muscles. Take your right hand from your heart and move it near your pelvic region (women—cover your ovaries and uterus). I want you to rock forward just a little bit, moving, swaying, gently, back and forth, just a little bit, back and forth rocking, breathing in energy and relieving stress in that part of your body.

You probably will notice where your body holds most of its tension while you are doing this—maybe in your back or shoulders. Let those areas relax. You should begin to feel a little heat going into your hand from your solar plexus. You will notice a little difference in the way it feels.

Now take your left hand from your stomach and put it right under the tip of your spine (your tail bone) under where you sit. Cup it there, breathe, and let go, breathe and let go. Feel the pulsations on your left hand as the energy goes through your body. (*pause*) Now, let your hands drop down to your sides and relax.

Breathe and let the air out through your nose. Hold your hands up so that the energy flows up toward the sky. Your hands will feel peculiar from all the energy. Your hands will be pulsating. This is the energy you have taken away from your body that did not need to be there. Imagine this unwanted energy leaving your body and disappearing into space. All the undesirable vibrations have left your body. Keep sending it upward. The marvelous light from the moon has restored your natural vitality. (*pause*)

Place your hands on the floor, palms down on the sides of your body. Get in touch with the earth's vibrations. Imagine that you have a golden rod coming down through your spine, running straight down into the earth, until it hits the center of the earth. Only you can tell when this is. Sit in the silence and you will begin to feel the earth move. You will begin to feel the vibration of the earth through your palms on the ground (floor).

You now have aligned your chakras through the earth and you will feel the earth's energy in your hands. Breathe gently. I will be quiet now while you absorb the earth's energy.

(*silence for six or seven minutes*).

Now put both of your hands on your chest, palms toward your body. Seep the energy into your chest, breathe it in, put some emotion into it, breathe the energy into the chest. Now everyone in the circle join hands. Ask the Indian woman spirits to join our circle. Ask them any way you like. Everyone now ask for an Indian spirit to come into your life, to help you, guide you, and direct you in the areas that promote healing and cleansing within your own sphere and family. Ask it to stay with you for at least a month to help you and guide you.

Now begin to see white light come out of your forehead into the center of the circle. Imagine it. See Mother Earth in the center of our circle with Mother Moon above her giving energy into the earth. Ask that all the people—men, women, male children, female children—be cleansed and affected spiritually, whether they be our new leaders or whether they need to learn about love and emotion. See energy radiating from all the women's bodies on earth, being sent out to all men on the earth. Feel them rejoicing in femininity and love. (*pause*)

Give thanks to all the things you would like to give thanks for. Thank you, beloved father, mother, god.

Full Moon Communication

This exercise may be done alone or with a close friend. Sit outside under a tree or around vegetation. If it is too cold, sit inside where you can see the moon. Stare at the moon in silence. Take time to reflect on the beauty of the moonlight and on the wonder of nature around you. Be appreciative of your life and of the marvelous light and the influence of the moon. Feel the power of the moon coming down into the top of your head. Enjoy the energy for at least ten to fifteen minutes.

Acknowledge the Moon Mother as an enormously powerful feminine entity. Begin to see her face. You may notice that her mouth seems to be open to answer your question or to give you advice. She specializes in affairs of the heart, feelings, creativity, spontaneity, and psychic abilities. Ask her for answers. Feel her light and warmth and watch her mouth move. Hear the answers she gives to you.

Morning Sun Chant

In the morning, go outside and face the sun. Take your drum or rattle. Face the sun and feel the warmth on your face. Do not look directly into the sun, but sweep your eyes under the sun for four or seven times. This allows the energy from Father Sun to revitalize your body through your pituitary gland. Beat your drum or use your rattle or hands to reach up to the sun like a bird in flight. Feel the reverence for the Sun Being that gives you light and life. Let the rays of the sun come through your palms and into your body. While using your instrument or moving your hands, begin to chant whatever comes to your mind. Do not analyze the sounds or words, just let them flow. You are giving thanks to the Sun Being, and he will give you a song or chant for your use. Let it happen. Most Native American prayers and chants were quite simple and repetitious. They often repeated phrases four or seven times during ceremonies. For example, a simple chant to the Sun Being might be: "Great Morning, Sun Spirit. See me here below. Give me power. See me here below. Take my pain. See me here below. Hear my plea. See me here below."

Put a simple melody to the words and you have a powerful prayer.

Setting Sun Chant

The setting sun provides another opportunity for prayer and song: "Setting Sun Spirit. Lay me down with peace. Take my enemies. Lay me down with peace. Give me rest. Lay me down with peace. A (man/woman) asks for you. Lay me down with peace."

Chapter Seven

Bushyhead packed his medicine bundles into a soft leather bag specially designed to hold sacred objects. He prepared to journey to his place of power. This was to be a special journey because Little Hummingbird would accompany him. For the next ten moons, he would teach her his medicine. Upon their return, he would announce the identity of his successor during a ceremony. After that time, Little Hummingbird would be known as Too Many Birds. This name, revealed by the spirits, would increase her power and changed her identity to a medicine woman. Before leaving his tepee, he prayed to the four directions and to the Great Spirit above and to Mother Earth below to help him with this tremendous task.

Since her full moon ceremony, Little Hummingbird had definitely become a woman. *She has a serious air about her—too serious*, he thought. Bushyhead grimaced when he contemplated telling her about Coyote Tooth and the death of her mother. How he wished this could be a joyful occasion! To learn the divine ways brought ecstasy. Why must earthly issues interfere?

Of course he knew the answer to that question. Through the drama of human relationships, one must learn important lessons and thereby reach higher levels of spirituality. If he successfully handled his earthly responsibilities before he died, his soul would not return to earth. This thought comforted him.

Bushyhead sensed that Little Hummingbird had many questions that needed answers. His time with her was precious, and extra needs and questions often went unanswered. Many procedures remained untaught and must be revealed. After presenting her to the tribe as his replacement, he planned to finish her sacred learning. His time to join the Great Spirit drew nearer with each moon.

Too Many Birds' power would protect her from Coyote Tooth after he was gone. It was up to him to see that nothing happened before that time, and he had been defeated before. Because he had been awakened by the spirits to his enemy, he felt confident in his ability to shield his granddaughter from all harm.

Before Bushyhead left Pumpkin Vine Village, he told the villagers that he planned to visit his sister, who had married into the Comanche tribe. He took Little Hummingbird with him. Fortunately, his people were on friendly terms with the Comanches, who occupied an area to the south. Therefore, it was necessary to leave the camp going a direction opposite from his place of power. Once safely out of sight, they would double back toward the north. They would have to take hidden paths and use lesser known trails, because it was important to keep the power location hidden. It would take them an extra day in travel time but Bushyhead planned to use the time to talk of important matters.

As they left the village, Coyote Tooth watched and then approached his son, Grey Badger.

"Many people, especially the young women, notice that you have not chosen a wife. From your actions, I detected a special interest in Little Hummingbird, and she watches you intently. Because you will become the tribe's medicine man, you will need a powerful and skilled wife like the granddaughter of Bushyhead. I will discuss the possibility with Aunt Morning Star if you are agreeable. You will learn many powerful secrets if you observe and question. I will begin now to teach you of healing and setting bones so that you will have all of my knowledge."

Grey Badger showed no hesitation in his answer. "I chose no wife because I waited for Little Hummingbird to have her moon ceremony. She is the wife I desire and I need wait no longer. However, the duty of medicine man for the tribe is the most important concern in my life, even more than marriage. In this case, the betrothal will further my skills. Yes, you have my consent to begin preparations."

The two travellers continued their journey. Bushyhead and Little Hummingbird wove in and out of foliage, shielding their presence from any hunters or warriors in the area. Bushyhead walked rapidly, and Little Hummingbird almost ran to keep up with his pace. She listened as he talked of sacred knowledge.

As you become a medicine woman, Little Hummingbird, you will notice that special events and opportunities will present themselves. Because Eagle guides you and because you have bird medicine, you will have many messengers with wings. They will both warn you and present you with coming events. You will develop a feel for the information.

Included in your medicine bundle will be feathers and eagle totems presented to you by your helpers. No doubt some will appear during this journey, and others will come to you as you need them. Keep them in your sacred medicine bag for the rest of your life. Powerful items will be left in your path. Keep your eyes open and your consciousness awake at all times and you will avoid many problems in the future.

No one must ever touch the contents of your medicine bag. It is to be kept in a sacred place in your tepee. The villagers will be afraid to steal it. It only needs protection from witches who want to take your power. For this reason, never leave it unattended when bad vibrations are around you. The bundle can be stored away for protection. When my medicine bag is not being used or safely stored, I wear it tied to my waist. My medicine bundle hands in my tepee on the west side, away from the door. Your grandmother performs offerings four times a day to protect and honor it.

Your sacred medicine will be used whenever you need to heal others and gain personal power. It will help you portend the future and obtain information.

The appearance of birds in unusual settings or close proximity is significant. Sightings or finding feathers or other power items happens for a reason. Be alert to the hidden message. Questions are often answered.

In addition to your lifetime medicine bundle, you will be guided to objects or herbs to assist you in healing or using power. You will prepare special medicine bundles for different occasions. To assist a mother wishing for a baby, you will use a lock of the mother's hair, a sacred corn kernel, a red stone, and herbs such as black walnut and red raspberry. The bundle will be wrapped in red string and tied to a bush with a feather so the spirits easily locate the offering. This is done at the beginning of the new moon.

The first night, they stopped at dusk. Both were exhausted by the extra energy that they had had expended by doubling back and keeping themselves hidden. Little Hummingbird listened to every word her grandfather said during their trek and had little energy left for more questions. Grandfather quickly prepared a fire for warmth and they both sat in the crackling heat in silence. Little Hummingbird broke out a meal of braided pumpkin strips and dried buffalo meat. Aunt Morning Star included a special flat bread made from corn meal and berries. This tasted especially good with honey, which came from a section of a hive stored in a leather pouch.

Little Hummingbird spotted a butterfly pupa hanging on the low branch of an tree over her head. The amber-striped larva sparkled in the final rays of the sun as it descended below the horizon. Mesmerized with the glittering tree ornament swaying in the orange twilight, she sat and stared. As she watched, an orange-and-black-striped lump began to emerge from the bottom of the transparent chrysalis. Finally a damp, crumpled butterfly emerged.

"Grandfather, look at the beautiful butterfly that has just been born."

Bushyhead stood up and walked over to where Little Hummingbird pointed. They watched as the monarch moved its wings up and down to dry them. The shaman said,

Nature reflects the activity around it, for we are all one in the universe. We are all brothers and sisters to each other. You watch your first butterfly emerge from its cocoon because you yourself will emerge as a medicine woman during this trip. This one is especially big and beautiful. Remember what I said about messages. This butterfly brings you an important message about your life. You will go through another period when you feel restricted and, perhaps, depressed. But you will survive your ordeal to become a glorious spiritual being with unlimited beauty and grace. Always remember this lesson.

Bushyhead returned to his place by the fire while Little Hummingbird reviewed the words she had heard. His message brought feelings of both fear and joy. Her mind went immediately to Grey Badger and her heart began to ache. Would there be problems with Grey Badger in the future?

"Do medicine women marry, grandfather?"

"Yes, my child they do, as I have married as a medicine man."

She hesitated before asking the next question. "Did your wife ever fear your power or show jealousy? I never saw any sign of it in my dear grandmother."

"There are times, Little Hummingbird, when you will be misunderstood. Your loved ones will expect you to have more power than you do to help them or they will feel that you have used your power to take advantage of them. Such is a shaman's lot. My wife and I solved the potential of bigger problems by always talking of the subject openly. Even though I could not reveal certain procedures, I always answered questions about my influence concerning any family member. Your grandmother trusts me as I trust her. With that trust, you can overcome all obstacles."

"Will I marry, grandfather?"

Bushyhead looked surprised, as if the subject had never entered his mind. "Of course, little one. Your ability to love others will attract someone with the same ability to you. You no doubt will have many to choose from, for you are beautiful and full of spirit. Why would you ask such a question?"

"Oh, grandfather, I worry whether a man would be afraid of a woman with power."

Bushyhead reassured her. "A man would welcome a medicine woman, because it would greatly increase his own power. Even medicine men search for powerful women. What man would not want more magic?"

Seeing the fear subside in her eyes, Bushyhead suggested that it was time to restore the body through sleep. "Even though our spirit bodies are busy at night, our physical body must rest and recuperate. I hope that I have removed any fear of jealousy from a future husband. Remember the butterfly emerging from its confinement. Do not harbor any fears of your future wellbeing, for the butterfly emerges victorious. Now sleep, my child."

105

Little Hummingbird suddenly found herself unable to sit up any longer and sank down into her bed of leaves that were covered with a buffalo-calf skin. She could smell the freshness of the damp earth and moss. The sky was clear and she could see all of the stars glittering in the sky. The stars were ancestors of their people who, through great deeds, had earned their place among the spirits. At death, the soul faced alternatives. It could go to the Land of the Dead at the end of the Path of Souls (Milky Way), or it could become a ghost and remain on earth. Everyone hoped to join the Spirits, because to transform as a ghost meant an afterlife of torment.

Her mind drifted toward the story of the foolish girls who wanted to have Star Men for lovers instead of choosing from the men in their tribe. When they reached the heavens, one girl found her lover too old and the other girl found her lover too eager. Both wanted to come down from the sky and rejoin their tribe, but they were too lazy to weave ropes. Instead, they offered to have sex with numerous animals, if they would help the girls get back down to earth. Finally, Wolverine agreed, but carried them back up into the sky because he wanted to keep them. The girls got away by persuading Wolverine Woman to take their place in secret.

Little Hummingbird drifted off to sleep when her eyes became too heavy to remain open. She dreamed that a young man lay with her, her head cradled under his well-muscled arm. He spoke of love while the moon shone behind him in a halo of soft light. In the dream, a fire burned behind her, increasing her feelings of warmth and wellbeing. The dancing flames highlighted the gold sparkles in the young man's eyes as he leaned closer to her.

As his face approached hers, she heard the roar of a strong wind that pushed them apart. A whirlwind surrounded them, scattering ashes and hurling them in different directions. She reached out for the man as he was swept away, bewitched as if in a trance. She cried out for him but he floated off, seemingly unconcerned. Finally he was thrust upward in a spray of sparks from the fire, his eyes looking up toward the clouds. Above the fire, she saw the image of a coyote's face, his cheeks puffed out as he blew the young man higher and higher.

Awakening in a sweat, Little Hummingbird sat straight up and looked around. Other than her vision, which had proclaimed her power animal, Eagle, she never remembered having such a vivid dream. It was as if the dream was as real as life itself. She realized that the man had looked like Grey Badger, right down to the gold flecks in his eyes.

Aware of the implications of the dream, she stayed awake feeling fearful. She felt her skin crawl when she heard the hoot of a nearby owl. *Yes,* she thought, *there was no doubt that something was wrong. Maybe, Grey Badger was in danger!* Little Hummingbird knew there was nothing she could do so far away. Before her return, she would ask her grandfather for advice as to how they could help Grey Badger. She didn't want to bring up the love dream with him, for she believed it made her look foolish, like the lazy girls wanting Star lovers. She was here to learn sacred medicine, and earthly matters were out of place.

Unable to return to sleep, Little Hummingbird lay watching the evening star move toward the horizon. Overhead, she noted that the new butterfly had not yet left its chrysalis. It hung onto the small remnant of its former shell as if it was not yet strong enough to attempt flight. In the moonlight, she saw its slow fluttering as it dried its new, wet wings. *Perhaps tomorrow,* she thought, *it will venture out on its own.*

MEDICINE BAGS

Each medicine man or woman possessed a medicine bag made from animal skin that contained power objects for healing. The contents of each bag varied in size and number, but most contained bird or animal bones, tails, feathers, or claws and an assortment of herbs or roots, smudges, paints, rocks, or other symbolic articles to represent a deity, such as the sun. Of supreme importance, even more than the contents of the bag, was the song each shaman possessed. The song was sung while the medicine objects were being used during ceremonies. The song, given by the spirits, was the catalyst for releasing powers.

Today, we have only the animal and bird body parts, which are more or less dropped on our doorstep. The contemporary medicine person does not need to kill for food and would never capture an animal or bird for his or her medicine. If you are truly walking the Rainbow Path, personal power objects and opportunities for feathers, and even dead birds, will appear. Dead birds and wild animals appear in a synchronistic fashion to a person, much as the live ones do.

Road Kills

One source for feathers or skins are "road kills." To be prepared for road kills, always travel with plastic bags, a sack of salt, a sharp knife, gloves, sage, a small shovel or trowel, and a paper bag for burial.

When you see a dead creature by the road, pull over safely off the road and examine it. The first items found for your bag may be the most important ones and will be lifetime power articles. If it is a bird with wings both folded in toward the body (instead of at least one wing sticking out away from the body), if it is badly decomposed, or if it is a skunk (rabies carrier), leave it alone. If the specimen is not decomposed, and you have a feeling it was meant for you to find, you have two options.

First, you can put on your gloves, place the animal or bird in your plastic bag, cover it with salt, and take it home. If it is a dead owl, eagle, or other protected species, decide whether you want it in your car. You cannot prove it was hit by a car before you found it.

Second, if you wish only the feathers from your specimen, use your knife to cut away the two wing sections and one tail section, put them in your plastic bag, cover them with salt, and put them in your car trunk. When you get home, select a cardboard box large enough to spread the feathers attached to the wing. Cover the bottom of the box with a layer of salt (you will need a large amount, and pickling or regular salt, which is sold in bulk, are good choices to use). Spread out the wings in the cardboard box. Place a thick layer of salt over the entire wing, including the feathers. The salt will preserve the wing by drawing the moisture out of the meat. Leave the wing in the salt for at least six weeks. Do not cover the cardboard box. Leave the wing in the salt until there is no odor. Remember, once dried in place, you cannot rearrange the feather spread, so they must be placed as you want them.

Small animal skins (separated from the body) may be temporarily covered with salt, until the proper curing procedure is performed. Kits may be purchased if you wish to do it yourself. Small animals can be taken to a professional curer. Large animals should be left where they are found after a blessing of sage and a prayer to hasten their journey toward the Rainbow Path. Always use gloves when handling dead animals or birds.

Small animals or birds can be buried in a paper sack, using your shovel. Sprinkle sage before covering them and ask that their journey be a good one. Leave undesirable animals (decomposed, etc.) where you found them, untouched, with a sprinkling of sage, if desired.

Contemporary Medicine Bags

Because we may not have many wild animal skins and parts for our medicine bag, we add more stones, crystals, and amulets to them instead. Feathers are important, and as mentioned, you will have many opportunities to find them.

Most medicine bags today are used by an owner to increase his or her own spirituality and sacred power. Medicine used for manipulation of others will inevitably come back on the user. It is permissible to increase your own power *for the good of all*. If you have an important meeting where you wish to present yourself in the best possible way, take your medicine bag with you in your briefcase or pocket where it cannot be seen. If you are in a conflict situation with another person, use your medicine bag for power but always make it clear that the outcome you desire from your power is *for the good of all involved*. In other words, use your power to better yourself, not to defeat another. Always check your motives and ask that others be considered.

On the Rainbow Path, many objects will come your way that will interest you or seem significant. After discovering your power animal, you may find small carvings or statues of this particular creature and others may give you feathers or stones. Put these in your medicine bag. They may be important power articles. Eventually, you will have collected so many items that it will be necessary to choose only the most significant—the space in your bag will be limited.

Helpful items such as cornmeal, sage, and herbs are often placed in a secondary bag. In addition, larger items, such as rattles and large feathers, can be wrapped in larger bundles. Drums and blankets are handled singularly because of their bulk.

Sample Medicine Bag Contents

Feathers from power birds or birds

Animal skin, whole or partial

Crystals (type depends upon need)

Stones (type depends upon use)

Fetish (purchased from a Native American—usually a carving—may depict a power animal)

Jewelry (if contains special stone or is symbolic)

Amulet (These are symbolic, may be a cross or other religious object)

Special insect or butterfly (in tiny bag)

Any item with special significance

Occasionally, a piece of jewelry may be taken out of the bag and worn. However, except for stones, which are changed as particular needs are desired, the rest of your bag should remain intact and in a safe place. It should be small enough to be placed in a large pocket but ample enough to hold your supplies. The best bags are made from soft animal skins fashioned by Native Americans. Do not buy objects decorated with animals skins unless you feel drawn to those particular items, because it promotes trapping and killing. You will have ample opportunity to obtain animal articles.

Each item in your medicine bag is representative of sacred power. Each item is essentially a talisman. It reflects the power of its owner, a person, an animal, or a community, just as the American flag reflects the essence of America.

POWER BUNDLES

A medicine bags remains with a person throughout his or her lifetime. Even today, many Native American tribes have community power bundles carefully guarded by select persons. These bundles are opened only at special times and the contents are considered sacred and untouchable.

Today, individuals can make their own power bundles in two different ways. The first is to compile a large bundle using one's totems and sacred objects. This type is usually prepared during crisis situations or in times of need.

The second type of power bundle is small and is buried in Mother Earth or hung on a tree or bush. You do not see this offering again. You present this bundles as a request for certain favors and for powers to be received. For increased energy, bundles are presented or buried during certain celestial times, such as the new moon, the full moon, the shortest day of the year, the longest day of the year, the day of the first thunderclap in the spring, the day of the summer or winter solstice, of the fall or spring equinox, or of a solar or lunar eclipse.

If you wish for quick results, prepare your power bundle during the full moon. If you want help developing a new project, bury your power bundle at the height of the new moon. If you wish to ease your pain because of an ending relationship, choose a lunar eclipse or waning moon. The spring equinox is a good time for planting seeds and for beginning new lives and projects. The fall and winter help transformation and the severing of old ways and attachments.

The bundles in your possession are kept until either your wish is granted or the situation in question is resolved. These bundles contain articles similar to the smaller offering bundles except there is no limit to the number of articles that you can use. They are disassembled when desired, but the contents are retained.

Power Bundle Materials

Natural cloth (choose from five colors: black, white, red, blue, and yellow.)

Red twine or string

Cornmeal and tobacco

Sage, juniper, and cedar (You can substitute a local smudge for one of these, such as sweetgrass, red willow, carrot root, piñon, or mesquite.)

Lock of your hair

Strip of paper with your wish on it

Symbol representing your wish (picture, article, name)

Small rock or stone

Small totem to give away (for offering bundle)

Totems, stones, crystals, jewelry, photographs (for larger bundle)

Power Bundle Directions

Cut your cloth into six-inch or eight-inch squares for offering bundles and any size desired for the larger bundle. Different tribes used different colors to represent the four directions but they almost always chose from one of the five colors mentioned previously. Skins, leather, or suede can be used in place of the cloth for the larger one.

Tie each small bundle with red yarn after its contents are added. Use only a pinch of your herbs or offerings and choose small items. Tie your larger bundle with either a leather strip or red yarn.

Write your wish on a strip of paper and enclose it. Your wish must be specific as to the action desired. If the wish is "feminine" (creativity, love, receiving), add cornmeal. If the wish needs "masculine" energy (logic, aggression, analytical thought), use tobacco. Use both, if you want both energies. For the other plant offerings—sage, juniper, and cedar—it is permissible to substitute one plant that is native to your area.

A lock of your hair is always enclosed. For an offering bundle, add a gift of a tiny mineral or pebble and totem that you like, such as a small feather, a crystal, a flower, or a souvenir. Add a symbol if you have one. For example, a health wish might include a picture of yourself in good health or a wish for a raise might include play money or a sketch of your boss handing you a check.

Love wishes might include a valentine or poem. Fold these up so that they are small enough to fit into the bundle.

After your smaller offering is complete, bury it or hang on a bush or tree on the day you have chosen. Sunrise, sunset and the new or full moons are powerful times to offer your bundle.

A larger bundle, which you will keep, can include appropriate tarot cards. Add any additional objects to this power bundle, fold up, tie, and store in a place where it will be undisturbed.

Eileen Nauman, who has Cherokee ancestry, refers to the offered power bundles as prayer bundles. She presents her bundles to Mother Earth for burial or hangs them on a bush or tree. She says that your first four bundles are the most important. She suggests using four different colors to represent the four directions and using the color appropriate for the wish.

She uses black for north, yellow for east, red for south, and blue for west. Put the request for business direction or power in a black cloth. A wish requesting change or transformation goes in a blue cloth. A yellow cloth, representing the east, is appropriate for a request for ideas, for creativity or for beginning projects. Requests for money or love go in the red cloth of the south.

Make your first four prayer bundles for yourself. Do one for each direction. After two weeks, you can make bundles for other people at their request. Nauman smudges before she does a prayer bundle. She always asks Mother Earth for permission to bury the bundle. She digs a hole, puts in an offering of sage, tobacco, juniper or cedar, buries the bundle, and then adds more of the aforementioned offering before covering up the bundle. She adds a feather to any bundle tied to a tree or bush. The different bundles can be offered on the same night or spaced out.

Do not dig up your bundle or go out to check its condition. It will disappear when the wish is granted. You must be careful what you wish, because if it is right for you, you will get what you asked. Wishes cannot be retracted. Some wishes will be granted in several days, others will take several months. Give extra power to your bundle by directing positive thoughts and emotions toward obtaining your goals.

POWER RITUALS

The most powerful rituals are those accompanied by joy and celebration. Two ingredients must be present: emotion and action.

The action may be physical or it may be mental. Native Americans, as mentioned earlier, depended to a great extent on song and prayer for their power. It was believed that a song was given to them by the spirits, and it was what enabled them to have power. If you are serious about walking the Rainbow Path, then you will need to find your power song. You also will need prayers, which should be simple and uniquely yours. Those with the highest requests receive the fastest attention.

The amount of ritual performed by Native Americans would surprise most people. Some ceremonies last for many days, during which memorized behaviors, songs, and prayers were enacted. A Piegan (Blackfoot) Indian Beaver Bundle ceremony was reported to have had more than three hundred songs or repetitions that had to be sung!

The importance of ritual in obtaining power is overlooked in our society. Ritual quiets the mind, making it accessible for spiritual acts, and a quiet mind blocks out negativity and wasted energy. Spiritual songs and prayers give power to the person performing them. The power of thought control used in a ritualistic act was known and practiced by the Native Americans.

For example, the words, "power, powerful, it is powerful, I am powerful, they are powerful, her medicine is powerful, the smudge is powerful," are used in Native American ceremonies. By repeating the words, their energy is released. Remember, Native Americans used such words to ask for attention and blessings from their spiritual helpers. To be granted the power, you must request it from your supernatural helpers and ask that it be used for the betterment of all. To use your power for anything but the highest aims will result in problems for yourself. The stronger the power granted, the more repercussions you will suffer if it is misused. Beware!

Empowering Yourself and Objects

To increase the intensity of your energy and to empower objects with vibrations, use the following rituals:

Smudge yourself and place an object so that it faces one of the four directions.

Turn and face each of the four directions, both standing and bowing.

Shake your rattle above your head and below your waist in each direction.

Blow tobacco smoke (or offer tobacco) above your head and below your waist to each direction.

Say a prayer to each direction, above and below.

Sing your song to each direction, above and below.

Dance your power animal in each direction, above and below.

Burn smudge toward each direction, above and below.

Offer cornmeal to each direction, above and below.

Now face the object toward the next direction and repeat each of the above steps. Repeat until the object has been blessed in each direction. Each time the object is moved, repeat the words, "I am powerful, this (*name the object*) is powerful. My medicine is powerful, the (*name the object*) is powerful."

Suggested articles to empower are personal objects, totems, feathers, crystals, stones, and jewelry.

Power Song

You can find your power song by yourself or with the help of a drumming group. Burn sage or incense and listen to a drumming tape or beat a drum yourself. Then, with your eyes closed, let yourself get totally relaxed and concentrate on the beat. You will eventually hear words or music that will form a rhythm. Let yourself go and experiment with the words or tune. Sing it over and over until you remember the sequence. Let yourself sing whatever comes to mind. All you need are several phrases with a melody. If doing this in a group, anyone receiving a phrase or song should sing aloud spontaneously, then wait for another to find his or her song. The song that comes to you may be your power song.

Do not let others know your song except during a medicine gathering. Remember the song and write it down. When you need to use your medicine, sing your song. If you cannot sing aloud, sing to yourself. Use this song whenever possible. It will gain in power as it is used.

Chapter Eight

At sunrise, Little Hummingbird began her prayers to the morning sun. She asked for blessings and especially a powerful memory to remember the words to the songs and rituals that Grandfather had taught her. While he continued to sleep, she collected firewood to cook the breakfast of cornmeal mush. She walked some distance away, so as not to awaken Bushyhead. To awaken a sleeping person, except in song, was to disturb the part of them that travels among the spirits during dreams. If not given time to return, part of the soul might decide to stay in the Land of the Dead.

She picked out some small pieces of wood and started to take part of a log, when she noticed that it was the remains of a tree struck by lightning. One never used such wood, for to do so brought on "staying sickness." As medicine woman, she would treat many cases of this disease, which is brought on by not treating certain objects with respect. After her mother's death, there was speculation that Wounded Deer had witnessed the killing of a rabbit while she carried Little Hummingbird. Some thought that this caused her death. However, Grandfather disputed the theory because Wounded Deer didn't mention any such sight to him. He believed that if such an event had occurred, she would have asked him for medicine to overcome the consequences of her transgression.

A mockingbird called to Little Hummingbird from a tree and jumped down on some broken limbs that were just the right size for firewood, causing them to fall to the ground for her to pick up. "Thank you, my friend," exclaimed Little Hummingbird. She noted that this bird followed Bushyhead even on his travels.

I am a lucky person, Little Hummingbird thought. *A bird to find the wood to cook the mush and a grandfather to start the fire.* Bushyhead had the magic to start fire with his hands. He had only to touch a small kindling stick and it would ignite. He rarely did this except for ceremonial purposes. Several times a year, he used this talent at festivals or ceremonies, and once a year when the tribe met with the Pawnee, the medicine men from different clans put on a display of their magic. Grandfather started fires at that time, but only with wood set in front of his hands so that you could not tell how he did it. When he traveled with Little Hummingbird, he needed no dramatics. He merely reached over and touched a stick to make fire appear. Bushyhead told her he felt she'd be given another magic talent, but he did not have the power to give her his fire skills.

He told her that all magic comes from thought control combined with the highest spirituality. What you think, you create. When thinking or conceiving is done with absolute faith, a pure heart, and emotion to set form to the thought, all things can be created. She remembered a Pawnee medicine man who could create rabbits out of thin air and thought of others who could produce tobacco from their palms.

Grandfather told her that she could materialize anything if she thought about it enough. As her power increased, she would be able to bring about effects. It would be obvious to her at some point that she was creating her own reality.

The hardest lesson for anyone, including those with medicine, is to learn to control thoughts. You must never think destructive or negative thoughts. Think only pure, loving thoughts. What you think you will become. What you focus on, you bring to you. What you fear will happen to you. What you want you will get. Because you have medicine, all these truths will happen tenfold. You have the sight and the wisdom, and those who possess and do not use these gifts suffer more than those in ignorance. A shaman has greater distances to fall. To achieve miracles, you have only to meditate and pray for them to happen. But, you must know that the miracle will happen, for any doubt will cancel its creation.

Again he reminded her that meditation or concentration on negatives would also bring that result. Bad miracles are created by witches purposely using bad medicine. Good shamans must be careful what they think, for they can bring harm to themselves and others. Their power comes to them from the spirits, and it must be controlled. Her grandfather went on.

Do not attach yourself to possessions. Possessions become dust that clouds our perceptions and our sight. If attachments become burdens, give them away. Time spent in worrying about loss brings bad vibrations and loss of power.

Never tell another person what to do, or suggest to them that you know more than they do. See others on a destructive path as learning their lessons in the way they have chosen. On the other hand, to not tolerate abuse of children, animals, or helpless people.

Returning with the firewood, she found her grandfather saying his prayers and singing his song to the morning sun. He would teach her this and other songs during their visit.

As her grandfather started the fire and she prepared the breakfast, they watched a butterfly fluttering around the camp area in search of nectar. It stopped to drink some dew on a leaf through its long, tiny, tube-like tongue, which was kept coiled up underneath its head when not feeding or drinking. Then it landed on a mulberry that was decomposing on the ground. The monarch tasted through the tiny hairs on its body, and smelled through its antennae.

Later, when Little Hummingbird and Bushyhead prepared to continue on their journey, they saw that the butterfly already had left. On the way to their destination, the old man sang and the young woman listened. Then the student sang while the teacher listened, and afterward both sang together. It took the whole day to sing the songs Bushyhead used in his ceremonies. He assured her that she had memorized them well. "The singers and drummers know the other ceremonies and will perform those while you make medicine," he told her.

The next day, the travelers reached their destination as the full moon appeared in view over the horizon. Grandfather chose this time to teach Little Hummingbird because the Moon Mother would help to teach her the sacred ways and during this time was at the height of her powers. As they slept in the shower of her soft light, Little Hummingbird felt a mixture of excitement and sadness. It was an exciting time for her, for she was to be blessed by the highest of spirit helpers. But, part of her wished she could remain eternally a child with her dear grandfather, listening to his wisdom whenever she needed it.

During their time together, Bushyhead told Little Hummingbird of the sacred ways. For three days, they did not eat or sleep, but prayed and practiced the many rituals needed by a shaman. When she felt that she could not go on, the old medicine man told her not to worry, the spirits would teach her in her dreams all that she would later need. All that she had to do was ask them to take over. Eagle would come when beckoned and perform the ceremonies, as long as she furnished the body.

He also told her secrets of health and old age. "Do not say everything you know. Just use as few words as you can to convey your message. If you talk too fast and too much, it will use up your life. You will have few enemies if you treat your dissenters with respect, but never underestimate your competitors' ambitions. To do so could end your power or your life. Always quietly observe them and take the necessary precautions to protect yourself in vulnerable situations. Do not ever give your power away in thought or action, for they surely will use your show of weakness against you.

"Do not be alarmed, my child, by the change in my appearance during the coming months. It will soon be the time to meet my spirit guides at the end of the Path of Souls. They have been kind enough to allow me this extra time, so that I could train you in secret. Now, I must reveal other problems. I talked of enemies because you already have one. Coyote Tooth covets the shaman position and will bring harm to you, if he can. He killed your mother because he thought she would inherit my medicine. You must avoid him and use your power to protect yourself against him, for he plots now to find your weak spot as he found mine."

Little Hummingbird's eyes widened in terror and her tan skin blanched white.

"Why have you not told me this before?" she cried.

"My child, you were too young and fear lowered your

119

power base and protection. Now you have no fear of being vulnerable."

Little Hummingbird slumped over as if in pain, unable to continue walking. Bushyhead helped her sit under a pine tree, where the ground was covered with needles and cones. Her grandfather could not understand her anguish.

"You are quite safe, little one. You need not worry."

Tears streamed down her face as she gazed up at her bewildered grandfather. Choking on the words, she stammered, "Grey Badger, son of Coyote Tooth, was my intended husband. I love him and always have. Now I cannot have him, for his father plots to hurt me. Oh grandfather, what will I do?"

Bushyhead realized he had been outwitted again and the pain of resignation etched across his face. Through her tears, Little Hummingbird thought she saw the flutter of beings with large white wings swoop down over them, but when she blinked, they were gone.

"Oh my child, what have I done? Why do I have these blind spots in dealing with Coyote Tooth? Never have I been prepared to handle the situations that he presents." He reached out and took her in his arms. "Now you, too, will be dealing with the same issue and much pain will come your way because of it. Let us pray to the Great Spirit for guidance." He reached in his medicine bag and took out his rattle. He began to shake it in the four directions and then above and below.

"Oh Great One in the Heavens, hear my prayer. Answer my plea for help and guidance. I have failed to protect my beloved granddaughter from the pain of my enemy. She loves Grey Badger, the son of Coyote Tooth. No doubt Grey Badger also loves her but is being manipulated by his father. We need a vision of the future to know how to deal with this troublesome situation. Hear my lament! Grant this request!"

As they kneeled together, lightning flashed over the mountain and dark clouds streaked across the sun. The wind swirled and picked up small leaves and branches and hurled them here and there. Dust covered their bodies and pine needles pricked their faces. Shielding their faces, they peered out from underneath their shared blanket as the spectacle unfolded.

120

From a distance, a small black cloud gathered force and grew bigger and bigger as it headed toward them. Thunder-beings appeared as a pack of huge wild horses running across the sky, their hooves kicking up the clouds behind them like dust on a parched trail. Bushyhead and Little Hummingbird smelled the musty odor of the dust clouds as they rolled by. It became difficult to breathe as the air became choked with sand and thick, grey air.

The pack came closer and closer until Little Hummingbird and Bushyhead could feel the air that the horses snorted in huge puffs of steam. The two lead horses approached, a huge white stallion with a black spot on his head and a mare. The mare was smaller, but her black body glistened irides-cently like the rays of the moon across a lake. The pair raised themselves up on their hind legs towering over the medicine man and medicine woman. The two clung together, not knowing whether they would be trampled under the hooves of the spirit horses.

Stopping, the two lead horses turned toward each other and briefly nuzzled. Then, the stallion veered sharply away from the black mare, his ears cocked as if listening to a far-away sound. Another mare, one with black and white spots, broke from the herd and ran to take her place beside the stallion. As they turned and galloped south, the shamans saw that the new mare's belly was swollen with foal.

The small black mare pranced and pawed the ground, her head dipping low, then raising up, as if signalling the pack for action. Finally, she galloped off to the west with the herd following behind her.

As the vision left, the wind subsided and the surroundings returned to their previously peaceful state. Only the film of dust, the scattered branches, and the fallen leaves on the ground revealed the reality of the vision.

Little Hummingbird found her grandfather with his head bowed in prayer. She could not wait for him to finish.

"What does it mean, grandfather? Oh, tell me what it means!"

"My child, you first must tell me what you think, because it is when we are stricken with grief that our visions are the hardest to interpret. This will be a valuable lesson for you, however painful."

121

She spoke softly with sadness in her voice, instantly realizing the message of the vision. "I was the black mare, as medicine person for the tribe. I turned west toward change and transformation. The white stallion was Grey Badger. He, too, is a leader and headed south where he will be involved in physical matters," she gasped. "He will take another woman as his wife, impregnated by the fertility spirits to lure him away. Coyote Tooth will have no power over me for his son will choose another."

Bushyhead continued for her. "Yes. He will be called to another tribe to set a broken bone and while he is there, he will be lured to another. He too, will become a medicine man and join the tribe of his wife, setting bones like his father and perhaps more. When I announce you as Too Many Birds, medicine woman to the tribe, I will say he also will be a medicine man and will learn from Coyote Tooth to heal and set bones. Later he will . . ."

"What about me?" she cried. "I will lose my love forever!"

Bushyhead dried her tears with a rabbit skin as he spoke. "Many men will want you as a wife. The vision stopped in the near future. You will know more later about your future husband. Be patient and wait. This man was not meant for you. Learning to handle loss may be one of the trials you must undergo in order to allow your own power to develop. Remember that you had some questions about Grey Badger accepting your power. You may have known that this man could not have done that. If you married Grey Badger, many obstacles would have drained your power and your ability to help others.

"Let your pain widen your perceptions and broaden your capacities. All true medicine people undergo trials of death and pain to test their faith. Let it be and trust in your own power to overcome all challenges. Many shamans have physical crises that almost kill them. Your test will be of the heart, which may be more painful. After it is over, you will have much power."

The last night before they departed for home, Little Hummingbird awoke in a cold sweat, in pain and terror. She must not only lead the tribe, but do it alone! She wanted to wail and cry with all her might but did not want to hurt her grandfather. She knew that he suffered greatly for her. Once, when she glanced at him, she thought she saw his eyes watching her. But after she blinked, he appeared to be asleep. Oh, how she hoped he slept, for she did not wish him to see her in pain and cowardice.

On the way back to Pumpkin Vine village, both shamans were silent. The knowledge had been given, the spirits had spoken, and both knew what they must do when they returned. They loved each other and soon, they would be physically separated when Bushyhead died.

Little Hummingbird watched her grandfather age before her eyes. Time seemed to etch his face and body by the minute. His strong healthy form shrank to that of a fragile, stooped old man with a wrinkled, kindly face. His eyes still sparkled but they looked out around a nose suddenly too large for the face. The skin hung slack on his cheekbones.

As if reading her thoughts, he spoke. "Do not be alarmed by my appearance or by happenings in the coming months. I will tell you before I join the spirits. I am thankful that you will be safe and will help our people. We have much to be thankful for, my child. Now I no longer can call you my child, Little Hummingbird. From now on, you will be known as Too Many Birds."

THE MAGIC OF THOUGHT

One of the best kept secrets is the power of thought. You create that which you think. Thinking of someone or something actually creates a thought form that is sent out into the atmosphere. This is the secret. Thoughts are matter.

The Native Americans realize the power of prayer, for to pray is to put thoughts into words with intensity. This increases the density of the matter that makes up the thought form. This matter in turn attracts particles on the same vibratory level, continuing to build until the object is formed or materialized.

If you think with emotion, thought particles form faster and travel greater distances. Unfortunately, negative vibrations, such as fear and hate, attract and materialize faster because the intensity of emotion strengthens the words or idea. The more emotion in your thought or wish, the more likely it is to materialize. For this reason, peaceful or beautiful wishes and thoughts must be accompanied by sincerity and love to speed them on their way toward formation.

Early settlers and European visitors to America did not realize how religious the Native Americans were. Because their rituals and customs differed, the spirituality of their nature was overlooked. Although time spent in ceremony and prayer differed between tribes, religion and deity communication occupied an important place in each Native American culture. Their traditional spiritual leaders stressed the importance of honor, power, faith, prayer, sharing, and community.

Their priests, shamans, and leaders recognized the power of a humble manner and of dedication to prayer. They sent requests out into the atmosphere for help and guidance. They asked for assistance from their spiritual helpers, knowing that their prayers would be heard and hoping that their requests would be honored. Intensity of emotion and sincerity was always present, along with self-sacrifice and honor.

In many ways, their levels of spirituality exceeded those of other groups. Today, the recognition that humans are all sisters and brothers to each other and to the other creatures on the planet is gaining widespread acceptance. It is no accident that Native American philosophy and techniques are being sought by those wishing to learn or to receive higher spiritual blessings in their lives.

Many tenets of Native American religions are similar to those of the major religions of the world, especially the Eastern religions. Although philosophies of the afterlife varied from tribe to tribe, the notion of being one with the universe and the acceptance of a great spiritual or vibrational power present in the essence of humans past and present, was found in most Native American religions. Today, many of the spirit guides and angels that help the planet appear in Native American form. It may be only fitting (given the white settlers' treatment of the Native Americans) that many people today who are interested in Native American religious beliefs are of Western European ancestry.

Other religions recognize the importance of thought, both in content and process (what you think, as well as how and why you are thinking it and the accompanying emotion). Some people believe that this is the key to all higher religious experience.

Native Americans have been characterized as circular thinkers, which allows one's spiritual essence to be more effective (being more concerned with living in the present, feeling what is happening around you, and experiencing the *now*). This is the opposite of linear thinking.

Theda Starr, a Pawnee, is a psychologist and healer. She is a natural therapist and profoundly affects others as she works. Her philosophy in healing is "unraveling one's life, and knitting it back together." She works to define the problem, change the defenses, increase understanding, and then to knit it all back together. She says, "Just begin anywhere—it all needs fixing."

Theda Starr believes that thought is prayer. What you think is essentially a prayer, because it releases energy. If more people were aware of this profound idea, they would be more careful about what they think.

Love, honor, patience, charity, faith, wisdom, and power are universally considered virtues to be cultivated in thought and deed. While most Americans are familiar with the philosophy of positive thinking, few know how to put it into action. But, before you can enact thoughts which become prayers, you must rid yourself of unwanted mental clutter.

Changing Thought Patterns

Before changes are made, first one must identify the theme or scripts one thinks about during his or her day.

1. Set your alarm at different intervals to catch yourself thinking, then record your thoughts on the left side of a piece of paper. Across the page, opposite your thoughts, record the general theme of your thoughts. For example, if you find yourself thinking of paying your phone bill at 1:00 and thinking of finding the money for new shoes at 1:15, both thoughts are different in content but have the same theme—concern about debts or money. You have a preoccupation with financial security.

2. If you are currently dealing with a crisis or problem, then you are aware of where some of your thought energy is going. Although you know where you stand on the subject, you may not be aware of the nature of your thoughts or thought processes or of the specific fears running through your mind. The more fearful or traumatic the situation, the more your unconscious fears and old habits take over. It is necessary that you identify these ruminations before you can successfully change your way of thinking. Use the alarm or write down your repetitive thoughts. What is the theme or underlying concern or fear?

Since most of us are not natural healers, especially in changing our unconscious habits, the writer lists a plan of action.

Healing Yourself

The formula for healing yourself is:

STOP—LOOK—LISTEN—TAKE ACTION

Stop!   Stop thinking the unwanted thought. Say "stop" to yourself.

Look!   Look specifically at what you were thinking.

Listen!   Listen for the underlying theme. What are you afraid of? What is the emotion behind the concern? Watch particularly for fear, anger, despair, jealousy, suspicion, resignation, pride, and need for escape. Has there been self-sabotage, carelessness, erratic behavior or laziness in your actions?

Now it is necessary to take *Action!*

ACT
   I (inner faith)
   O (own up to your responsibility in the problem)
   N (now let go)

ACT Take action by saying aloud:

"*I* have faith in myself, my higher self, and my heavenly helpers, to seek out what is best for me."

Own your part in this worry. "I did _____ and this caused _____ ," or, "I permitted _____ to do _____ ," or, "I chose to be with _____ "

Now, let go. "I _____ (your name) let go of worrying about _____ . If needed, I will take a specific action, but I will let go of thinking about this."

See and feel this problem, person, or situation floating up into the sky surrounded by white light. Now it is gone. If you find yourself thinking or worrying about this same situation repeat: "_____ (your first name), *let go.*"

Practice getting rid of worries and concerns that keep your mind cluttered with problems. Remember: *Thought is prayer.* When you keep your mind focused on problems, *you bring more of those problems into your life.* You attract the same vibrations that you send out. Change your thoughts or prayers to bring only good things into your life. Repeat the preceding exercise until you change your unconscious thought patterns. Do not be discouraged. Some sages spend their whole lives perfecting their thinking. If you begin to have more dreams of problems, know that your plan is working. For as you rid yourself of fears during the day, your unconscious will attempt to bring them back at night! This will last only for a night or two before your unconscious begins to change its conditioning.

Now that you have obtained some control over your thoughts, you can begin to insert higher thoughts and ideals in your daily thinking.

Materializing What You Want

Sai Baba, the great Eastern Indian religious leader, produces articles from his hands through thought. He has materialized hundreds of articles of jewelry, prayer beads, and sacred ash to people all over the world. Drinks Water, the famous Lakota Sioux medicine man, produced articles such as food, tobacco or matches as he needed them just by thinking of them. Helene Blavatsky, author of *The Secret Doctrine*, once materialized a cup and saucer to match her set when she needed one to serve another guest.

While you may not achieve these feats of materialization, you can accomplish even more important ones, such as changing the events that will occur in your life. Start now. By dwelling on several important ideals or emotions, you can begin to attract these qualities to you. Once you have weeded out many undesirable worries, fill that space with thoughts and ideals that can change your life. Bring love, protection, opportunity, goals, blessings for others, and needed goods into your life by thinking of them.

Self-Improvement

Analyze the qualities you most need or wish to cultivate and list them in order of preference. Start with your weakest quality. Then take this quality and think the word whenever you eat or drink during the day. For example, let's say you have the most trouble enjoying yourself. Think *joy* while you take a bite of food or drink something. Also, feel *joy* while you think it. This will help insert this quality into your subconscious and also attract it to you. Think this quality during the day, as the last thing before you go to sleep, and during the first five minutes after awakening.

Analyze the negative qualities most often present in your thoughts or behavior. Keep in mind the list above under *listen*. Select one negative attribute. Once a day, when going to the bathroom or showering (getting rid of unwanted bodily effects), picture this quality leaving your body at the same time. Feel it slough off your body, getting rid of it totally. Imagine it gone. After you have mastered that undesired quality, work on another. Choose the more powerful negative qualities to conquer first.

Substitute Positive for Negative

Negative qualities also can be countered with positive ones. For example, if you have a tendency to be depressed, think joy whenever you get a sad feeling.

Stop! When you catch yourself thinking and feeling a negative thought, such as a bad thing that someone did to you, stop.

Look! Now look for and substitute a desirable or needed thought and feeling in the place of the one that you removed, such as forgiveness instead of resentment (feel the substituted thought).

Listen! Now listen to yourself saying the positive word or phrase such as "I forgive _____ ," (and feel it).

In addition to the positive traits that you wish to acquire, other phrases and wishes may be used as affirmations. Some examples are:

1.   Repeat inspirational or religious phrases such as: "In God We Trust. Love Thy Neighbor as Thyself. Glory to God in the Highest. Peace on Earth, Good Will to Men."

2.   Substitute a thought or wish for a needed happening or article, such as "Heal _____ (name)" or "Provide money for my _____ (needed article)."

3.   Devise personal affirmations such as: "I am getting healthier and healthier, "I make the right decisions," and "I allow myself to receive love."

4.   When certain items or situations are needed, be specific in your requests. For example, say "I need patience when I attend the closing next Wednesday." If your whole life seems to be desperate and you wish for divine intervention, make general requests, such as "Thy will be done. I will accept what is best for me," or repeat prayers such as the twenty-third psalm, which begins "The Lord is my shepherd, I shall not want."

Thought Control

The more control you have of your thoughts, the more effective you will be in manifesting what you want from life. The following are some exercises to help you gain more control.

1.   Follow your train of thought for ten minutes. Do not analyze your thoughts, or try to focus them in a certain direction. Just follow your mind wherever it goes.

2.   Now, try to think of only one thing for ten minutes. Decide what single sentence or thought you want to concentrate on, and do so for ten minutes. Do not let any other thoughts intervene. When they do, push them aside and go on.

3.   Now empty your mind for ten minutes. Clear your mind totally. Look at the clock when you begin. At first you only may be able to do this for a minute or two. Keep practicing until you achieve a ten minute interval.

4.   When you can do all of the above exercises, you will be able to achieve lofty spiritual goals and manifest a better life.

Joy Walk

One of the best ways to practice daily affirmations is to incorporate them into a joy walk. As you enjoy the outdoors and observe nature, you can insert some words or phrases of affirmation. Feel joy as you say them.

After you have enjoyed the silence of the outdoors, begin to chant your new words and phrases of joy. A melody may come to mind. Sing it to yourself if others are around. Put your intense desires and highest spiritual needs to the melody. Time it in rhythm to your step!

Your joy song will differ from your power song as you deliberately will compose the words to become an affirmation for needed development. The power song may have only a few words and is developed from the subconscious.

You will want to sing your joy walk song during your walk, when you are driving, or when you are at home. After the song becomes automatic, your unconscious will be ready to help manifest that which you desire!

Chapter Nine

The entire tribe gathered for Bushyhead's important announcement concerning his successor. As medicine man, Bushyhead would consult the spirits for further information during a special ceremony before he revealed his replacement.

The council house filled with villagers, who seated themselves in a line with their backs to the walls. Mothers held small children, who had learned to remain silent for long periods. Infants in cradle boards were left in one tepee with a woman to take care of them. There could be no sounds during the ceremony.

All indoor tribal ceremonies took place in the council house, which was round and large enough to accommodate the whole tribe. There was a hole in the ground directly in the center where the animal spirits from the lower world could enter. The fireplace surrounded this opening. A space was left in the roof above it to allow the spirits from the upperworld to come and go. All other openings, doors, and crevices in the council house were sealed in order to make it as dark as possible. The Night of No-Moon was selected so that there would be less light, which would enable the spirits to enter without being seen.

After the ceremony, there would be a large feast. Bean and corn stew had already been prepared and enough buffalo had been roasted that the whole tribe could eat all it wanted. This was a very special occasion, the first in the eighteen Long Snows (years) that Bushyhead had served as tribal shaman.

The tribal chief, the elders, the honored warriors, and the drummers sat in a circle in front of the rest of the tribe. Bushyhead sat in the center. The firekeeper sat outside tending the fire, and from a kettle an honored woman served a ceremonial drink which was passed around for all to taste. A special puppy was sacrificed and added to the brew. The person who scooped out its head was assured of special favors that year. Only one scoop of the ladle was allowed per person. Fire In The Leg, a man of great speed, was the lucky winner, and his wife struggled to contain her pleasure as he demonstrated the head to the group.

As the ceremony began, everyone became quiet and motionless. Two elders came forth as Bushyhead lay himself face down on a blanket. They bound his hands and feet behind him. They they rolled him in the blanket and then in a giant buffalo hide, which was secured with many ropes. The drumming and chanting began. For the next hour, Bushyhead would journey to distant spirit worlds to gain knowledge for the tribe. Everyone knew it would be his last journey from his earthly home.

Too Many Birds sat with the women and younger men, who were leaning back against the council house walls. She felt strange, realizing she would be the only woman who would have a place of honor in future ceremonies.

The eyes of the villagers noticed the sparks beginning to twinkle around the dark room, a signal that the spirits had arrived. The sparks were like little flashes from lightning bugs, only smaller, quicker, and with no definite pattern to their movement. Occasionally, pebbles thrown by playful spirits clattered down the sides of the house. The tribe had grown used to these happenings. The purpose of the ceremony was to call the spirits and allow the medicine man to journey to a faraway place for information.

Too Many Birds felt a feather brush her cheek and knew that Eagle had joined her. She heard a few startled grunts as people in the group experienced movement around them. It was not uncommon to be touched or to hear sounds during the ceremony. The woman next to her felt fur brush by her arm and Too Many Birds, with her special vision, saw a squirrel spirit scamper over her and perch on one of the support beams.

After a long period of strange and unexplained events, a rattle sounded. This was the signal that Bushyhead had returned from his journey. The signal brought the fire keeper from outside. He undid the outside closing, removed the extra wrap to screen out light, and came in with a torch to light the fire directly below the smoke hole in the roof. As he started the fire, Bushyhead could be seen walking around and shaking his rattle. The spirits had unwrapped and untied him and he walked around to honor the spirits from the four directions. The members of the tribe always whispered and nudged each other when they saw him walking around, free of the ropes from which no earthly person could have escaped.

Too Many Birds saw the shape of Bear extending beyond Bushyhead's physical body. Bear's snout extended past the old shaman's face. His body was much larger than Bushyhead's although his movements coincided with the shaman's. It was as if Bear had become one with her grandfather, even though his physical form was much larger.

Looking around, she saw Grandfather and Grandmother Spirits sitting in the room, intermingled with the elders. The Buffalo Woman stood next to Bushyhead, who was surrounded by his other power animals. Other spirit animals frolicked about the room. A pack of wolves chased each other.

Too Many Birds gasped when a spirit deer approached her, its beautiful eyes like melted pools of brown topaz in the fire light. As Too Many Birds watched, the doe became a tiny woman who looked just like her. So, her mother was present at this event! She reached out to touch the spirit, but it faded immediately.

Suddenly her fears of the distant future turned to happy anticipations of the meetings she'd have with loved ones. She would get to rejoin her grandfather, her mother, Wounded Deer, her grandmother, and yes, even Grey Badger. For now she was certain the spirit lived on after the physical body died.

She spotted Grey Badger sitting across the room, with a tall Indian spirit guide behind him and a short guide with an animal face to his left. She could not tell what animal it was, perhaps a future power animal for him. It seemed that his life would be guided by spiritual beings, too. She wished him the best, even if they had to be apart. Her thoughts stopped abruptly as Bushyhead spoke.

"I will die in three moons." Sounds of surprise resounded throughout the room. "My granddaughter, Little Humming-

133

bird, now Too Many Birds, will take my place as medicine person for this tribe. Grey Badger will begin to learn from his father so that he may heal and set bones. He, however, will be called by the Fox Clan to serve as their medicine man in the future. At that time, Too Many Birds will help him secure secret knowledge after he has been ordained by the spirits."

At this information, Too Many Birds felt like a knife had been pushed through her heart! She would not only lose him to another woman, but had to help him do it! Yes, there was no doubt this was her trial of death. The anguish and grief must be conquered in order to prove herself as a shaman.

Bushyhead began to pray loudly to the spirits, thanking them for their information and allowing him to journey with them over the years. He asked them to inform him when it was his time (Ho Hota Hey—It is a good day to die). Then he said, "Let us celebrate. We have much to be thankful for."

It was several days before Bushyhead and Too Many Birds sat down to discuss events. Both had the feeling that the other was not eager to begin the necessary conversation. Bushyhead asked her to meet him at the great boulder to the east of Pumpkin Vine Village, a place of power where they could talk without being disturbed.

He spoke first. "My granddaughter, you always will be my child, but now I must call you Too Many Birds, a title of great distinction, for you are now officially a medicine woman for our tribe."

"Thank you, my grandfather." She spoke in a new, deliberate, mature tone of voice. "I work on preparing myself for your death when the time approaches, but I will need no help with the mourning wails that will come from my mouth and heart. As you stated, it is my fate that I must experience the loss of my loved ones and help them through the transitions, as I will do with you when I preside at your death ceremony."

Bushyhead looked at her with empathy. "Yes, Too Many Birds, I was not eager to tell you the news revealed to me by the spirits. You will help Grey Badger learn medicine. I knew the pain it would cause you because you were aware he would have new surroundings and a future wife. Trust me, medicine woman, when I tell you that it is for the best and you will reap many rewards in other ways. These trials of grief and loss will propel you into the heavenly world of the Star People after this life.

"The loss you experienced at birth was an omen of the future happenings that you would experience to gain power. Although you lost your mother, you have had your grandmother and me to love and help you. But challenges come in cycles and it is time now for an important time in your life. I will die and you will become my successor. Grey Badger will leave but you will find another. I know nothing about your future husband because he has not yet been revealed.

"It is through the experience of loss that you will conquer your fears and become a powerful medicine woman. On my journey to the Star People, I saw many things that I could not reveal to the tribe. You will become a Star Woman with all the privileges. You will have a happy life in the Path of Souls. You can also choose to join earth people if you wish to help someone on his or her path. For this, you will resume another earthly body and have all the accompanying pains and pleasures as you work to gain even higher status in the stars. As you continue to help others, you will be promoted in the hierarchy. I will be there, too, as I will remain in the Path of Souls teaching spirits like yourself.

"Grey Badger also will be there, so apparently he will escape Coyote Tooth's influence. In fact, Coyote Tooth has only a short time to live, because I saw him dead in the snow this coming winter. It appeared he was caught in an animal trap he had set, forgetting its exact location because of the snow. When he went to look for it, his leg was snared and he froze to death in his own trap."

Too Many Birds could not prevent herself from asking the question. "If Coyote Tooth dies, why must I lose Grey Badger?"

Bushyhead answered quickly, as if he knew the question was coming. "Because your destiny as been outlined and your future power secured because of his loss. You were to meet him and then lose him as surely as the Morning Star comes up in the morning. Do you understand?"

She spoke quietly, "Yes, wise one. I understand but my heart has not yet accepted its loss. Please tell me more of the spirit world for I do not know all that I will need to help our people."

"Spirit life is as varied as life on the planet." Bushyhead looked into space as if he already had joined the unseen world. He continued. "Spirit forms from lower levels, such as primitive animals and evil people, do not occupy places in the heavenly world for they have not attained that privilege. Coyote Tooth's ghost no doubt will remain earthbound for years, maybe centuries. Eventually a higher spirit will give him another chance to prove himself through good works in another earthly body.

"Earthbound ghosts are troublesome. They interfere with those susceptible to them, sometimes taking over weak people and forcing them to perform deeds. Of course, Coyote Tooth would not dare threaten you because of your strong power, unless you give your power away."

Too Many Birds became disturbed at that idea. "How would I give my power away?"

"We give our power away when we let others take advantage of us, especially when we are in a weakened condition. Do not let others abuse you. Also, do not let negative emotions overwhelm you with fear and anger. If you remember these warnings you never will be in danger from the ghost of Coyote Tooth.

"Our people are aware of the dangers of ghosts and are afraid of even uttering a dead person's name or looking at his or her clothing. This is why we always burn the personal articles belonging to the deceased or give them to a nonrelative. Nonpersonal items that we keep are carefully smoked with sacred sage.

"However, most ghosts are friendly spirits who stay around only long enough to attend their own rites. Afterward, they are led by their higher spirit helpers to their destination in the Path of Souls. I do not attempt to differentiate them from the ghosts who remain as tormented souls wandering the earth. It is better that the tribe should feel that all ghosts are dangerous because they cannot make the distinction. This will allow the living on earth to be released from the deceased or his or her ghost.

"There are exceptions. Some friendly ghosts will continue on the Path of Souls only after their loved one can go with them and so remain earthbound with their mate. These souls can be as troublesome as their earthbound counterparts who *must* remain here. This is why I encourage my people to avoid ghosts and memories or possessions of the dead.

"These are the reasons we build a grass hut for those dying. For example, that way their tepees do not have to be destroyed and their ghosts stay farther away. All my clothing and possessions will be burned except for my medicine, which I give to you. I wish to be arrayed in my sacred bear claws and my medicine robe at death."

She spoke quickly. "Do not speak of death at this time, for three moons remain and I want to enjoy every moment I can with you."

Bushyhead looked frail and seemed to shrink in size by the hour, but kept a twinkle in his eye. "Too Many Birds, I'm afraid you will not lose me yet. I always will be available when you need me and will attend your healing ceremonies for several years. I will watch to see that you don't make any mistakes or hurt any of my patients. I will travel back and forth from the Path of Souls to Pumpkin Vine Village in my spirit body until I'm sure that you know what you are doing." With that he laughed and hugged Too Many Birds who now stood taller than her grandfather. She caught his mood and laughed with him while she held his bony hands, wishing she could stay in that moment of time forever.

THE UNSEEN WORLD

To see into the fourth dimension of the spiritual world, you should begin two processes. First, do everything you can to develop your higher spiritual self. Many exercises have been given in this book to help you begin your journey. Other printed materials abound at specialty bookstores. Reading about angels is particularly helpful. Seek out experiences that give you a sense of inner wellbeing and satisfaction. Take courses offered by local psychics and spiritual leaders and organizations that will help to develop your senses and your awareness.

Second, and more important, develop an intense desire to view the unseen world. After you have gained the motivation, you will begin to see, feel, and hear into that dimension.

Begin by tuning into your own feelings and intuitions. Trust your instincts and act on the knowledge you have in order to improve your life. You will being to notice different sensations as you change locations and company. Some places and people will give you a calm, pleasant feeling. Others will cause you to be uncomfortable. Homes will send out the vibrational level of their previous or current owners. Realtors notice that certain homes have cheery personalities but others, possibly with many owners, harbor bad vibrations. Pay attention to people, places, and things that give you a peculiar feeling.

Although you will not want to linger in uncomfortable surroundings, remember your reaction. Your vibrational level will attract or repel the energy around you. Individuals in panic or fear gather undesirable energies to them. You literally can make your fears come true by thinking certain disastrous thoughts. Unfortunately, most of what we think that we see in others is actually a manifestation of our own faults and hidden desires being projected. The one million women (men were rarely suspect!) children, and animals killed during the witch hunts were victims of such paranoia.

If you sense a negative atmosphere, you have only to avoid the places or people that make you feel uncomfortable. It is important to heed your inner sixth sense as it develops. Undesirable or nonspiritual people can drain your vitality and energy, which limits your higher spiritual development and progress. You can make yourself sick or choose a slow death by living with the wrong person or in an undesirable location.

Bad energies in the atmosphere are usually thought forms

(yours are around you more than anyone else's). Remnants of past thoughts or actions, ley lines (magnetic fields), and, occasionally, earthbound entities may have either positive or negative energy. Some ghosts are quiet pleasant and are unaware that they are not embodied. Begin to develop your sixth sense so that you will be more aware of the unseen world around you and choose the most desirable company and surroundings.

Spiritual people, churches, sacred ground, power places, and guardian angels emit a sacred essence. You will begin to sense these vibrational levels and feel their energy and power around you. Seek out and choose these experiences to increase your awareness of the higher planes of existence.

Your first experiences with higher beings may come in the form of seeing faint flickering lights and shadows during meditation or prayer. Seek solitude so that you can be more aware of their presence. Ask for them to come to you and ask for their guidance. You soon will be able to tell when they are near. Some people feel a certain temperature change, when they are around. Others can see slight fluttering movements on the walls or ceilings. Spirits move quickly, and occasionally a change of light or air pattern occurs as a result. It is usually when our eyes are unfocused or looking slightly to the side that we notice these patterns of movement. When we look directly ahead, it anchors our brain to the routine, third dimensional world that we perceive.

Seeing Auras and the Unseen World

One of the most common experiences when contacting the fourth dimension is seeing someone who has recently died. What is seen is their etheric or spirit body. This spirit body surrounds the regular, physical body and severs its connection with the physical shell at death. It extends about an inch from the physical person, and is visible only to certain people. However, the ability to see it can be cultivated by you. One of the best ways to begin communication with and awareness of the fourth dimension is to notice the auras surrounding bodies.

Seeing auras requires practice and perseverance. Although individual abilities vary greatly as to skill and to practice time required, most people can learn to see the etheric or physical aura around a person. With much practice, the emotional aura, which surrounds the etheric aura, can be viewed. This is especially true of higher spiritual people, whose auras are quite bright and pronounced. Viewing the mental aura, which extends a foot or two out from the body is harder and usually requires a great deal of practice and effort. The spiritual aura surrounds the mental aura and is the most difficult to see.

The best times to practice are those when you are seated for extended periods, such as during a class, a church service, or a meeting. The classroom, with its green or black chalk-board behind the instructor, is an excellent place to attempt seeing auras. If your teacher's aura has red in it, you'd better complete your assignments!

Churches are even better. Although the minister or priest is not in front of a blackboard, his aura is usually well defined. If you have the opportunity to be around other religious figures such as holy people, medicine men or women, shamans and other healers, you may note an easily visible aura that surrounds their head like a halo. In some cases, you will be able to see an aura going all the way down to a person's feet. If the emotional aura is dark instead of light, you have chosen the wrong teacher.

Ceremonial occasions, such as powwows, weddings, and funerals, are excellent opportunities to read auras. They often have the added presence of spiritual beings who bring their own essence to the event. Be sure to look for angels as well as the etheric or spirit body of the deceased at funerals. This spirit body is sometimes called the astral body. The deceased will usually attend his or her own funeral, because the astral body remains on the earth plane for four or five days or more before ascending upward to the astral plane. This spirit body of the deceased is often accompanied by angels, who will aid him or her in a future ascent.

Put yourself into a relaxed state by taking deep breaths. As you watch the ceremony, unfocus your eyes slightly to the side of the people involved. At powwows, look between the drummers or dancers for spirit helpers. They will be dressed for the occasion. Look for transparent shadows that move independently of objects around them. During medicine gatherings, look for shadows that have feathers or resemble animals.

At special church services and funerals, look for angels. They appear as luminous shadows with large extensions (these may be wings) on the side, forming the shape of a cross. They are large and are sometimes seen standing next to the wall of the church in front of the congregation. They often stand next to the spirit body of the deceased at a funeral. The deceased's astral body should be standing close to his or her favorite person, invisible to all except those with the sight. The average spirit body will appear as a faint, life-size shadow, which is sometimes easier to see if you are sitting at least twelve feet away. The angels are more luminous and larger.

Auras are composed of some of the same essence that makes up the spirit body. Auras, however, contain colors that reflect the physical, emotional, mental, and spiritual aspects of the living person. The astral, or spirit body, no longer has the physical body with its accompanying chakras, but it does retain the emotional, mental, and spiritual components, which it takes to the astral plane.

Auras are seldom of just one color, although they can be. A spiritual person giving a talk may start out with a yellow aura and end up with a bluish purple one, as he or she switches from an emotional state to a more mental-spiritual one. Sometimes a holy person or spiritual channeller will have purple, white, or blue colors in his or her halo. Many of the colors in auras change with the type of activities and thoughts. However, people do seem to operate generally out of the same chakras and as a result give off several main colors. You will never see a purple aura on a criminal, for example.

If you want to practice reading auras, do so at work or in a meeting in which you are seated among people and can stare unnoticed at the back of their heads. Or, you and a friend can practice on each other. Use sage to smudge yourselves and the room or burn incense in the room close to your bodies as an alternative. Take deep breaths in through your nose, hold, and breathe out through your mouth until you feel slightly lightheaded. Take turns standing up against a white, cream-colored, or very dark wall and examining each other's auras.

The easiest aura to see is the one around the head because it is the brightest and the person's clothes don't obscure the view. As with the rest of the body, the etheric aura is first and extends a little less than an inch from the head. The emotional aura is next, ranging in width from two or three inches to a foot from the body in highly developed folks. The mental body extends out a foot or so from the emotional and the spiritual aura several feet from that. Buddha's spiritual body was supposed to have extended for a mile! So you see there are many variations in the size of the spiritual body and few people in our lifetime will be able to see this aura. You can work for years to perfect your skill in reading the easier-to-see etheric or emotional auras.

When you attempt to see a person's aura, do not look directly at him or her. Unfocus your eyes several inches to the right or left of your target area. If you are examining the etheric body, which is close to the body, gaze several inches away from that position. If you are examining the astral or emotional body, you may want to focus some six to eight inches away so that you can pick up the whole span of this aura which averages around three to four inches from this body. Experiment with training your eyes on different positions of the body.

Try looking at your own aura in an untinted mirror. Look to the side or above your head and stand back from the mirror until you have the best light for viewing. Do not stand beneath a bright light. Sometimes, a side mirror will help you to see the aura from a different perspective, but this is not necessary.

Be persistent and continue to stare off again and again until you pick up the aura. As you turn your eyes to get a better look, you will find that it disappears! This is where patience is required. Do not get discouraged, because eventually you will find that the "sight" becomes easier and requires less time and energy. At first, it may take an hour of practice to get some elusive glimpses that last only several seconds.

Remember that each of the auric layers requires a different focal point because it varies in width from the body. Beginners usually focus on the etheric first, because this is the easiest aura to see.

The etheric or physical body is only an inch or two from a person's body and duplicates its outline like a shadow. A healthy person will have a light, luminous etheric aura. A dark or hard-to-see aura indicates physical problems in the body. The etheric aura may balloon out instead of keeping the form of the body. A dark spot in the aura indicates illness. For example, if the aura around the head is dark, it might indicate mental problems, or depression.

Next, attempt to view the emotional aura. This aura, once detected, will appear in color and is reflective of a person's emotions. While there is some disagreement as to interpretations of shades and hues, most seers generally agree that the purple and white auras are reflective of spiritual persons of high caliber. An indigo aura indicates a person in a higher mental or spiritual state. A blue aura indicates an intellectual. Depending on the clarity and hue, this could be either a controlled, restricted person or a person with a high degree of integration of the mental and spiritual self. Yellow reflects emotion. The pure yellows are love and devotion, the green-yellows may reflect jealousy and possessiveness. Interpretation of green in the aura varies with hue and clearness. Muddy green may mean a controlling, stingy person. A clear emerald green will indicate either a strong dedication to a cause or an organized life. A great deal of red in the aura may reflect anger or passion.

Reading a person' emotional and spiritual nature from auric color is for advanced students because many mistakes can be made. The auras change as a person's emotional, mental, and physical states change. The auras will be somewhat different on certain parts of the body, reflecting the condition of each chakra as well as physical and mental problem. The aura is a dynamic, flowing, pulsating aspect of a person. The different colors will flow together, blend, and separate as influences in parts of the body come together or are overpowered by each other. When you see an aura, you are only observing an aura at one particular time and place, and for this reason you are subject to your own perceptual errors. Sometimes colored clothes reflect into the person's aura and give it a false color. The head aura is usually the easiest to see and subject to fewer errors form the interpreter. In addition, it is the best indicator of the subject's inherent nature.

Beginners should not concern themselves with color at the start. The first step is to see some light or shadow around the body. Always make sure your background or lighting is not giving you shadows in the room. Unfortunately, the backgrounds are not always helpful when it comes to reading an aura. It is best to practice with friends against plain walls. Babies make good subjects because their bodies and minds are still unaffected by environment. A baby may almost glow in the dark. A sleeping baby may be observed at night without his or her objecting.

Chapter Ten

The early morning sun burst out over the mountain peak, bathing Pumpkin Vine Village with golden rays of light that sparkled and danced across the snow covered terrain. Greeting the sun was Too Many Birds, dressed in fur-lined moccasins, buckskin leggings, and a tunic covered by a large buffalo robe. She knelt by the river, praying to the Sun Being for help and guidance in the day's healing ceremony. As was her custom, she prayed facing the river between two boulders that shielded her from intrusion on three sides. Willows offered privacy from the back.

Facing the east, she began her prayers just as the first rays of sun peeped over the mountain. She thanked the Sun Being and the Great Spirit Mother for giving her the inner peace that she felt. Her days of grieving and loss were over and she faced each day with a tremendous joy in her heart. She asked for help in her healing work, which she greatly enjoyed. Today she would heal a child with an unknown ailment that kept her weak and sick.

Too Many Birds had performed healing ceremonies for more than a year now. Even before the death of Bushyhead, at the end of last year, she had begun healing those in need. There had been the warrior wounded in a confrontation at Crooked Beaver Pass. He had been hit in the shoulder with a tomahawk, which had crushed the bone and damaged muscle tissue. Grey Badger had already left to assume the position of medicine man for the Fox Clan, so she had had to heal the warrior herself.

Her grandmother showed her the proper herbs for healing bones, and she also used warm compresses of clay and herbs. Too Many Birds advised hot river baths in the steaming water that poured into the river from the mountain. Over the years, villagers had placed rocks around this area in the river so that it stayed hot even though the cold river flowed on by.

After the bath, he was to mix clay and herbs to make a new compress for his shoulder and then lie in the sun all afternoon. To help the healing process, the warrior began wearing a turquoise necklace over the injury.

This treatment followed her first eight-day healing ceremony. It was necessary because of the high fever the warrior developed before he reached camp. It took her almost a week after the ritual was over to recover her own energy. The results surprised even herself. The man regained full use of his arm and shoulder and was now out on a hunting party, fully able to use his bow and arrow.

One of the last skills that her grandfather taught her was how to call upon Eagle, her power animal, to facilitate healing. As she performed the ceremonies, she asked Eagle to come into her body so that she could use his power. Eagle would also give her certain formulas for remedies as she needed them and would attend to the wounds during ceremonies. She always used the feathers and claws of Eagle when healing. The feathers, attached to two tiny rawhide strips, hung together from her headband to her waist. She added the claws to the turtle shell rattle given to her by Bushyhead.

She had also inherited the drummers and singers who worked with Bushyhead. They had medicine through their power songs and knew the order of the musical rituals. After she heard them, she realized that her talents did not lie in the rhythms of the drum music and chants, for without their signals she could not tell when the rituals would start and stop. There seemed to be no orderly sequence to the drumming but none of the four drummers, who also sang, ever missed a single beat together.

They "carried" the ceremony for her grandfather's funeral, for although she officiated she was in deep mourning and was too sensitive to remember the ritual. There was no need to make sure that Bushyhead's spirit body arrived in time for the ceremony accompanied by his Spirit Beings, because he had arranged it all before he died.

During the ceremony, all the members of the tribe had their hair cut in a special tepee. The woman cut their hair all the way around, but the men only cut the right side of their hair. Then, all the clippings were gathered together and, during the ceremony, taken to the river to be given to the River Spirits. Ordinarily, only relatives performed this ritual to speed their beloved's spirit to the Path of Souls. But because Bushyhead was their medicine man and greatly admired all the villagers participated in the hair-cutting ceremony. His clothes were cut into pieces and donated to the fire during the wake to show further respect.

Bushyhead had asked to be laid to rest as far north as possible in the village cemetery in a location where his platform would overlook his power mountain and because he was so loved, no one complained about the long trek to his resting spot. He was dressed in full medicine man regalia, with his bear claw necklace and the full feather headdress usually designated for chiefs. The crying ceremony lasted for a week. As Too Many Birds had predicted, she needed no encouragement for her wails of grief. It was as if every unmourned disappointment and loss in her young life was commemorated as she grieved for her beloved grandfather. But she was also reassured by the appearance of Bushyhead's spirit body, which acting just like he did in life! She knew that she would rejoin him one day. But she reflected on the fact that she would not be able to hug and touch a spirit body and so she sorely grieved.

She stayed with grandfather after the honored warriors and elders had deposited his body on the platform and everyone had returned to the village. She wanted one last visit with his physical body. She knew she never would return to this spot again for the main cemetery was out of view of his location. She wanted to remember him clothed in his majestic attire, as he was when she last visited with him. No one would dare disturb the grave of a medicine man, but she did not want to see his physical body again.

Too Many Birds recovered from her grandfather's death quickly, owing to an incident that occurred three days before he died. She slept soundly that night because during the day she had helped harvest the pumpkins that would be pounded and braided into strips for the coming winter. Earlier, she rolled the pumpkins into a buffalo skin, which was tied and dragged back to the village. As she worked, she remembered that it would soon be the end of the three moon period that her grandfather had predicted as the time of his death. Too Many Birds welcomed the work as a partial diversion from this reality.

During the night, however, she was awakened from her deep sleep by the sound of her grandfather's voice. "Too Many Birds, wake up." Bushyhead was wearing his turquoise and bear claw necklace over his buckskin clothing, and he carried his medicine bag and turtle shell rattle with the turtle's claws and bear's teeth on it.

"Grandfather, what are you doing here? You should be in bed."

She thought perhaps she was dreaming the vision, so she rolled off her buffalo robe bed and sat up to see if he would disappear. When he remained in the tepee, she reached over to touch his arm, but her hand passed through his transparent spirit body. He spoke. "I must say good-bye to you now, my granddaughter, for I will be too weak to speak to you in my physical body the next three days. I want you to be prepared for that before it happens. Although I will be unconscious, I will hear every word you say to me. Do not be alarmed, for the Grandfathers and Grandmothers wait for me and I am unafraid. They will stand over me and wait for my spirit body to join them. You will see them but do not express shock for they are my guardian angels.

"Do not let others know what I have told you. No one else will be able to see my guardians. Do not mourn for me except in the crying ceremony so others will not think you have given your power back to me. I will appear to you at different times when I am needed. Do not tell your future husband of these visits, for it could interfere with your marriage relationship. Bear will remain in my special place of power if you ever should need his assistance. He will accompany you back if requested. You also can ask for me and, when I can, I will appear to you."

Too Many Birds wanted to plead with him to live, but she remained silent and motionless through his message. As she started to speak, he held up his hand and said, "I must leave now. Know that I will be well taken care of in the Path of Souls in the sky."

When she visited him the next morning, he lay unconscious in his tepee and remained that way until his death three days later. Remembering what he said, she talked to

147

him when the others except her grandmother, were out of the room, who also talked to him as if he heard. Too Many Birds wondered if she also knew he could hear her voice, but she said nothing.

Too Many Birds reassured him that she was handling everything properly and explained how she was doing it. She told him they would move him to the Hut of Sickness, before he died, so the tepee which grandmother loved would not have to be burned. They knew his presence would be strong in the tepee but grandmother soon would follow him and have no need to remove his essence for the remainder of her life. Too Many Birds doubted her grandmother would complete the "turning loose" ceremony before she died, and she was right.

Ordinarily, people who lost their mate would remain in seclusion until the relatives dressed them in new clothes and "turned them loose." They all would have one last cry, and then the person was free of all ties to the deceased. This period of time could last up to one year or more, but Too Many Birds's grandmother died three months after Bushyhead.

Too Many Birds remembered the instant of her grandfather's death. She saw his spirit body rise up and float over his lifeless physical form. The cord connecting the spirit and physical body snapped as if it were cut at the moment of death. Bushyhead smiled at her in his spirit body, but lowered his head, discouraging her prolonged looks. She reached over and tenderly touched her dead grandfather on the forehead placing an eagle feather over his eyes.

The cry of an eagle above Too Many Birds brought her back to the present time. *Thank you for the wake-up call,* she thought. Her knees ached from the position and she chastised herself for letting her mind regress in time instead of communicating with her spirit guides. She decided she was prepared to heal the ailing child and started to walk back to the village. She would perform extra offerings to the spirits and ask Eagle for help today. Because of the time spent remembering, she would not wash her hair before the ceremony.

As she passed by the honeysuckle bush, she remembered the happy incident when Grey Badger placed a blossom from

148

its branches in her hair. Again, her mind floated back in time.

She remembered when Grey Badger left Pumpkin Vine Village. He seemed so happy to be a medicine man and seemed eager to begin practicing. Yes, he was sad when they parted but he thought their separation was temporary. He did not know their relationship would never reach fruition. Grey Badger told her he would visit on the second full moon, but he never returned. By the fifth moon, he had married. She was surprised at her own indifference to the news but then she had mourned his loss many moons before. The actual happening seemed like old news.

Too Many Birds stopped by the tepee, which, given her status, she now inhabited by herself and gathered her medicine supplies. She selected certain stones and herbs for healing and picked out special sage and sweetgrass to burn. The child, whom she was going to heal, had a high temperature that would require white willow bark to break the fever and take away pain. She made sure to put a special yellow crystal into her medicine bag and gathered up some nettles to brew for a tea for the little girl.

Accompanied by Lonely One, she walked toward the council house where the relatives waited with the sick child. It was time for the healing ceremony to begin. As she approached the opening of the council house, she was greeted by a new drummer. It was One-Eyed Elk, the son of a former drummer, who recently had to retire due to weakening arm strength. She had known One-Eyed Elk since she was a child. He received his name at his vision quest when an elk, weak from hunger, approached him in the wilderness. He gave it food and water and used herbs to heal its eye. Since that time, he had great elk medicine. It was assumed that the elk that appeared to him was a spirit in disguise. After the incident, he had gained stature as the best hunter in the village.

Once inside the council house, One-Eyed Elk walked over to her. "I will be taking my father's place," he said. "He has taught me the songs. I am looking forward to watching you heal and to helping in the ceremony." He gazed a little longer than usual, but she was preoccupied with her task ahead and had little awareness of his interest in her.

149

During the ceremony, Too Many Birds used the shaking-hand technique to locate the problem in the child. She used the yellow crystal to locate the source of the sickness in the child's abdomen, then with the white crystal, carefully drew out the poison. She prepared the tea, adding echinacea to the nettles. While the tea brewed, she rubbed buffalo fat on the child's stomach. She then covered the area with clay and comfrey leaves. The child was soon soothed to sleep, and the ceremony ended. As the relatives left, carrying the sleeping child wrapped in a blanket, Too Many Birds noticed that One-Eyed Elk remained behind.

He waited until she started toward the council house opening before he spoke. "Too Many Birds, I was wondering if you would consider sitting with me at the Moon of the Snowblind festival here at the council house. I would like to talk to you."

Her eyes caught his look and a feeling familiar from another time and deep in her chest tugged at her. She started to offer an excuse, feeling much older than her seventeen years. But for an instant, she caught the brilliance of his aura, flaring white-gold in the darkness. She knew the goodness of his heart and she heard herself respond.

"Yes, One-Eyed Elk, I would like to sit with you at the Moon of the Snowblind. Perhaps we can talk more of the ceremonies before that time."

"Good, I will plan on being with you." He reached over to lift the covering to the entrance for her.

As his head lowered to the height of hers, she was sure that she saw stars glittering in his eyes.

HEALING WITH CRYSTALS

Crystals have been used by healers and diviners since humans originated. Each type of crystal has unique qualities and healing specialties. Virgin crystals handpicked from the mines are the best because they have had no previous owners and therefore no old programming. If you do not live in Arkansas or a state with crystal mines, then you can purchase one.

When you buy a crystal, it will have been handled by other people and will need to be cleansed of vibrations. Take your crystal and place it in salt water, made by adding a pinch of salt (sea salt is best) in a small glass of tepid water. Leave it there for a week for the initial cleansing and for several hours, or until it achieves its former clearness after every healing session.

Other ways to cleanse crystals, which are less convenient perhaps, are to immerse them in a running stream or ocean, bury them in Mother Earth, or smudge them well on all sides with sweet-smelling (high quality) sage. Those crystals not used for healing can be placed in direct sunlight to be recharged.

If you wear your crystal, you will notice that it clouds up after it has absorbed energies. Leave it in a salt-water solution until it becomes clear again. This will enable the crystal to continue healing with its energies at full strength. Crystals heal by sending out magnetic energy fields at desirable vibrational levels. Problem areas in the body have distorted or undesirable vibrational levels, and crystals help remove positive (undesirable) ions from the energy fields and substitute negative (desirable) ions.

Some experts believe that crystals amplify the energy around them if the energy resonates with the crystal. Remember that you have an energy field determined by your thoughts. Increase your power by using a crystal to help you broadcast your desires. Practice sending self-improvement messages while holding or wearing your crystal. The crystal also deflects undesirable vibrations and can break from the impact. The crystal can heal by sending out desirable vibrations and deflecting unwanted energies.

The crystals used most frequently for healing are clear quartz crystals. Usually the size should be at least four inches long with a well defined point. Do not buy a crystal with a broken point or end, because this is its antenna. You hold the crystal in your right hand with the point outward unless you are working on yourself. You always go in a counterclockwise direction when healing.

To program your crystal, hold it in your hand and give it a message or directive. You do not need to say it aloud. Just think it. For example, *please remove all positive ions from this person's chakras.* Or say, "I wish to feel joy today. I am going to fill you with the joy vibration and then wear you so that you will help me retain this energy." After doing this, feel joy going all through your body as you hold your crystal in your *right* hand, pointing it toward yourself.

You receive energy from your left side and give it out from your right side. Therefore, you always heal with the right hand. The left side is the feminine or receptive side and the right side of the body is the masculine or giving side. This is true in people who are left-handed as well as right-handed. Crystals can be used on chakras and problem areas or worn for increased wellbeing.

When healing others while holding a pointed crystal, always anchor yourself by imagining the healing energy coming from above you, through you and into the crystal and person. You do not provide the healing yourself, you channel the divine energy from above. This procedure does not deplete you and protects you from absorbing anyone else's vibrations. After healing and placing the crystal in salt water, flick your hands down to the ground, then rinse both hands in cool water. Feel all the unwanted energy leaving your hands and flowing into the water.

When wearing a crystal, select one that helps you accomplish your own healing. If you wear a small crystal with a point, the point should hang down toward your body. If you wear crystal jewelry, pick out a type of crystal that will harmonize with needed healing work.

Crystals that have been subjected to high heat in order to change their colors cannot be used to heal. Many stones are routinely radiated to change their colors. Some of these are amethyst, aquamarine, citrine, sapphire, topaz, colored diamonds, turquoise, and emeralds. If the color seems unusually bright, always ask if the stone has been heat-treated. It is not necessary to have bright colors. A pale stone, such as a light amethyst, works beautifully.

When worn around the neck, amethyst helps the throat chakra and brings spiritual thoughts to the mind. Worn over the heart, it protects and heals. This is especially helpful for people who work in high stress situations or for those in the health fields subject to the burnout syndrome.

An amethyst crystal used on the head chakras is powerful

enough to give you a headache if used too long. Do not sleep with a large amethyst crystal by your bed because it will keep you awake! This is also true for citrine crystal, which is yellow, or smoky quartz. The amethyst, citrine, and smoky quartz crystals are safely used in jewelry. They retain some power when cut into shapes. The large ones in crystal form are marvelous for increasing spiritual vibrations in your room and for promoting change and insights. They are known for their ability to help a person with a breakthrough, whether physical, emotional, mental, or spiritual. For lazy glands, use a citrine, amethyst, or smoky quartz crystal with a point to jolt them into action. To avoid tears in the aura, use sparingly.

Clear crystals with natural points are the ones used for clearing chakras and for general work on the body. Use the same crystal for the same task. Do not use one for healing one day and to increase vitality in the room the next day. Only use certain crystals for healing. Do not let other people use your crystals and do not wear or borrow another's stones. Crystals that are always used for the same purpose increase in programming and power. If you mix up their uses, you will scramble their computer.

For medicine, use your crystals for three main purposes:

1. Healing others or working on specific locations. Use a clear crystal with a point.

2. Wearing as jewelry with a specific goal for healing in mind.

3. Using as senders and receivers in a room or medicine wheel. For these, use the large crystals or rocks in natural form. Some of these have a beauty that is indescribable.

Uses of Healing Crystals

Quartz crystals (the best conductors and healers) are classified into two main categories: The glassy crystals and the dense or opaque crystals. Stones and crystals also can be a mixture of the two types. Amethyst can be either clear like a diamond or opaque. Cat's eye, jasper, onyx, and carnelian are types of crystals that are often opaque. Some healers believe the clear, glassy, quartz crystal to be the best conductor and healer. However, all stones have useful properties and thus you have a whole drugstore of mineral helpers waiting for you to use them. Incidentally, minerals and stones love to have human contact.

Minerals To Use In Your Medicine Bag:

Amethyst: One of the most popular stones, It can be expensive or inexpensive, clear or opaque, and can be fashioned into any type of jewelry. It is also found in crystals with points that are a foot long! How would you like to have that mineral friend as a helper? They are also found growing in round stones that are cut open to reveal the crystal growth (geodes) inside. Some of these, as well as the larger crystal stones, cost thousands of dollars. A polished, opaque amethyst may cost fifty cents. Use your amethyst for increasing your spiritual vibrations and for becoming more psychic. If you are one of the rare spiritual types who need "grounding," avoid this stone unless you are a healer. If so, wear a small amethyst over your heart for protection against burnout.

Rose Quartz: This quartz is pink or rose colored. It is an inexpensive helper stone. This stone is often found in a mass, such as a boulder. A large, pink quartz for your medicine wheel or yard will cost only a few dollars. This stone is often shaped into beads, which are used to make necklaces. The rose quartz necklaces that come down to your heart center are unexcelled for healing the heart chakra. Wear this stone when recovering from the loss of a loved one. Others who fear intimacy can wear this stone to open their heart chakra. Men or women who need this stone and do not want to wear beads, can wear a rose-quartz crystal with the point down. Have it set with some onyx on the side if you wish some protection while risking new relationships.

Citrine: A yellow- or gold-colored crystal that is often glassy in appearance and resembles a yellow topaz or diamond. It is not as well known but is one of the most useful minerals. Like the amethyst, it can be found in large opaque pieces as well as in tiny diamond-like gems. It is also found in crystal form with a point. Do not use the pointed crystal for healing as it is too powerful. Place it several feet from your bedstand so that it will not keep you awake, and it will help increase your psychic abilities and promote needed change in your life. This is the stone for students who need to increase their study skills and mental clarity. Wear it in shaped, jewelry form around your neck to increase your verbal abilities or wear or tape it on your solar plexus chakra to promote emotional growth—it helps to work through fear and anger.

Black Tourmaline: This beautiful stone is usually not found in bulk, and a small, unset stone may cost around ten dollars. This stone is unexcelled for providing protection against environmental stresses. It gives you more endurance in crisis situations. It makes attractive jewelry and can be worn as earrings or necklaces. To give you the most protection, wear a loose stone in your left pocket. This will block negative influences such as anger or fear from entering your aura. Black onyx is also effective the same uses and is frequently made into jewelry. For less expensive alternatives, use black apache tears or black or snowflake obsidian. These stones are readily available and provide excellent protection in traumatic situations. Include them in your medicine bag, which is hung on the left side of your body to provide a shield for your aura.

Red Jasper: This is an inexpensive stone that is an excellent grounding mineral. Carnelian is another red stone that provides grounding and is often used in jewelry. These stones are for those people who need to avoid amethyst. It will bring you right down to earth and help keep you focused. It is a must for disorganized people or those who procrastinate. All red stones are to be avoided by those people with serious physical illnesses or with manic personalities, as it can exacerbate these problems. Substitute hematite, flint, or petrified wood as inexpensive, nonstimulating alternatives. Healthy but tired or depressed people are those most likely to benefit from red stones.

Green Adventurine: Use this stone with another variety of quartz crystal, tiger's eye, to increase your luck in money matters. Always carry one or both of these stones in your purse, money pocket, or wallet, as close to the money as possible. Whenever you see it, think prosperity and this will program it into increased action. Use a larger stone of green adventurine or tiger's eye to set on your desk at your business location or any place where luck and good fortune are needed. These stones give you a good feeling just to look at them!

Other powerful green healing stones are turquoise, emerald, green tourmaline, and peridot, which are excellent for the physical body.

Beside the uses that I have mentioned, small stones can be taped to the body on specific locations, such as chakra spots or areas of physical ailments. Use more than one for greater effect.

For example, tape a blue azurite or amethyst to your forehead to increase your dreams or tape a citrine, amethyst , lapis lazuli, or sodalite on your throat chakra to increase psychic hearing and verbal abilities. Tape a small rose quartz to your heart at night for healing and any of the green healing stones mentioned above to your solar plexus to give you more self-confidence and to overcome fear and anger. Use a small carnelian, bloodstone, ruby, or red garnet to revive lost sexual energy.

All of these stones are to be worn periodically, as needed, and cleansed after prolonged use. The ultimate goal for a medicine man or woman is balance; balance in the chakras, and in the physical, emotional, mental, and spiritual bodies. Without this, energy cannot flow up and down your body and cannot be used to heal others. In addition, you cannot receive higher communications from spirit helpers if your chakras are not open to receive the vibrations. Blocked chakras will stop the flow of the vital, sacred energy that you will need for your spiritual journeys.

INDEX

ABOUT THE AUTHOR

Mary Atwood is a contemporary medicine woman. She has a doctorate in clinical psychology from the University of New Mexico, and is a practicing psychic and healer. She has studied under various Native American healers including: Theta Starr, Pawnee; Gary Bear Heals, Lakota; Ann Always In The Middle Shadlow, Cheyenne-Sioux; Robert White Eagle Browning, Comanche-Lakota; Eileen Nauman, Cherokee Metis; and anthropologist Michael Harner, Ph.D.

Dr. Atwood currently resides in Arizona and travels frequently to New Mexico, Oklahoma, and South Dakota to gather data for her next book and to teach Medicine Workshops. She was listed in the 1989–90 Who's Who of American Women.

NOTE TO THE READER

For those interested in contacting Dr. Mary Dean Atwood for a group workshop, please send a stamped, self-addressed envelope to:

Dr. Mary Dean Atwood
% Sterling Publishing Co., Inc.
387 Park Avenue South
New York, NY 10016-8810

A NOTE FROM THE ARTIST

I never make a complete statement in any painting, but I do wish to arouse the viewer to think and feel about the subject. I believe that every serious art work should create a reaction in the viewer but not be complete in all details. If it leads the viewer to react, think, or make a judgment, it has attained some success. The themes I paint are universal. There is a sense of being one with nature; that is part of my upbringing and it's at the root of all my work.

—Bert D. Seabourn, Oklahoma City